Priesthood and Ministry in Crisis

PRIESTHOOD AND MINISTRY IN CRISIS

Terence Card

SCM PRESS LTD

British Library Cataloguing in Publication Data

Card, Terence
Priesthood and ministry in crisis.
1. Clergy——Office
I. Title
262'.14   BV660.2

ISBN 0–334–00277–X

First published 1988
by SCM Press Ltd
26–30 Tottenham Road, London N1 4BZ

Photoset by The Spartan Press Ltd
Lymington, Hants
and printed in Great Britain by
Billing & Sons Ltd, Worcester

CONTENTS

PREFACE

My own quest for God, as far as I can know it, springs from longing for reality and depth to life, longing to discover meaning to unjust suffering (and so, in a way, healing) and a recognition of the need to live the one life each of us has as fully as possible.

I felt that the theological training I had as preparation for ministry following ordination could hardly have been better. The model of it was one characteristic of the late 1960s, which had trained many fine men over many generations and still continues to do so, though with modifications as a result of the many pressures and questions forced on the church – and by that I do not mean just the Church of England, of which I am a member, but all the Western churches. It satisfied my quest absolutely in a discovery of grace, God's free presence so to speak bringing me home in a way that could not have been more all-embracing.

On reflection I have discovered that that grace was from God as distinctly other than the ordinary and the human; not surprisingly, since I had not experienced such a presence in the ordinary and the human, lovely as they could be and often were. It may sound odd that I only discovered this later, but when you are completely in love it takes time and experience to bring you to reflect. Certainly there was still to be a lifelong quest – in ministry after ordination significantly in tension with another lifelong quest for people in the power of the same gospel – but paradoxically I could now rest and be satisfied with a bread from heaven joyful beyond words. Love had bade me welcome. The demand on me now was to remain disciplined in prayer and reading and the spiritual life, and so unmoved in my essentially godly calling, to live fully in the world yet with some detachment from it, and to work to pastor people, especially into church, so that they might also come to know that gracious God. Appropriately the theological colleges and their training, which enabled this typical experience of holy grace, were set apart from the ordinary and the human, and are largely so still. For this God who was my meaning was set apart, and is so still. All church life, in all its details, is naturally based on the self-same model of experience. Worship, architecture, teaching, Bible study, communal groupings, pastoring, training for today's church, mission and evangelism, freeing laity for ministry, fostering and recognizing vocation, authority and decision-making and deciding who actually should have the say, even the very details of administration, are based on this model.

Now I trust that it is quite clear that I have the utmost regard for the model of theological understanding and the experience of grace which I have experienced. From within the model I have had privileges of wide-ranging responsibilities and of entering into people's lives in the deepest ways. I too have been involved in the closest way with candidates for ordination, a concern particularly close to my heart. However, Christian and biblical tradition old and new clearly shows that this is by no means the only model, and in our time it is in deep crisis. There is a crisis for the ministry of the church, and when I speak of the ministry of the church I am not talking of abstracts but of particular persons like me, each with a personal sense of meaning. In the simplest terms, this crisis could be expressed in the most fundamental questions: 'What precisely is spiritual?' 'What precisely is grace?' 'What is the relationship of the spiritual to the ordinary and the human?' To put the crisis in another, more haunting, form: when we look for meaning, what actually is the meaning of meaning? And specifically, do theology and spirituality have eternally to be apart and so inevitably have to do with primarily individualized and inward salvation? Or can they rightly be social as well as individual in a more fully personal way? Indeed, can they be political? To this last question an increasing body of theology and spirituality is saying an emphatic yes which cannot be ignored.

The way in which Christian churches see themselves is being fundamentally shifted. The consequences of this shift will ultimately be a quite different church and ministry, but founded on an experience of grace every bit as spiritual. Such a shift will involve a costly discipleship calling for a re-examination of much of what has been accepted sincerely as Christian for modern times. Grace and meaning will have to be discovered, no longer apart from the ordinary and the human but right within it, particularly in the midst of disfigurement and sin and evil, going through those awesome things and out beyond in the hope of a salvation when one day God will indeed be all in all. At present we live in an in-between time when two times and cultures are locked in struggle. As we look to the future, this new model must be our meaning and the direction of our quest. I personally believe that the coming of this new model is inevitable. The critical question is whether we shall co-operate with providence in history.

Our age is perhaps one in which we speak of drama and crisis all too readily. However, biblical tradition, truly read, clearly interprets the life and history of humankind and creation as a whole as being critical and dramatic at particular points. I feel that our age is undeniably such a point. This will be my theme. Are the issues with which the church is struggling themselves the sign of a historical judgment on the church, an indication that it has itself become a blockage to the salvation for which creation is obviously crying out on every side?

In the churches, as in any group, such a crisis must centre most acutely on its leadership, those in priesthood or ordained ministry. This book will be looking at issues related to them. Most acutely there is the crisis of numbers which is being experienced in all the Western churches. How is this to be interpreted? Is it the inevitable consequence of the prodigality of our unholy times and a rejection of the eternally unchanging truths of God in the church, or perhaps an indication that the church which has always been truest when existing in changing forms in response to God's word in creation and its history has actually become fossilized in forms belonging to another time, which are now lifeless and unattractive? Is it perhaps that the image and model of the church's life as focussed in priesthood or ordained ministry has now to change fundamentally for the sake of the salvation of creation?

Integrally connected with the matter of numbers and the nature of ministry are serious matters like celibacy for Catholic priests, the ordination of women and the mushrooming throughout the world of a new community life often bearing all the marks of any Christian life worth the name, but which old church institutions cannot recognize as truly Christian. Then within Western society there is the serious crisis of identity for the clergy. After one has said that priests and ministers are there for God and church and people, how does one go on? There are other fundamental issues, most notably experienced in ecumenical dialogue and in freeing laity for ministry, but the ones I have mentioned above will provide enough major substance for this book. Together they will be shown to compel the conclusion that the churches, and indeed church and world together, are in an acute state of crisis precisely because the model of the church is no longer right, in particular the image and model of priesthood or ordained ministry which is its leadership. As for the struggle to free the gifts of the laity, it will emerge that it is the clergy themselves who are the perhaps unwitting but major part of the problem and the blockage. And all these critical issues, and all else they can be a sign of, are not, as I have already pointed out, academic ones, but bear upon real people.

There is a burden on the clergy which is particularly heavy because it saps heart and sense of personal integrity and credibility. The ordained minister can turn away from this special burden in various ways: the ghetto mentality, the hyperactivity, the anaesthetizing in different ways, the simple abandonment of the cutting edge of vision and going to sleep in the given structures, the 'renewal movements', and so on. Those staying with this special burden through this critical time will know a crucifixion indeed. The sharper the vision, the more harassing. It is scarcely surprising that the health of clergy is giving cause for concern, even if this is not publicly stated. And if a clergyman or his marriage should perhaps break down, this is sadly too often interpreted by those with pastoral responsibility as a sign of our times, of the pressures, loneliness, failures to relate, need for support, and so on.

Now while all this is true enough, I am arguing about something more fundamental, which lies at the heart of ministry itself; the model of its meaning and of the life and church it has to serve in the modern world. It is regrettable that there seem to be few voices in the church, particularly among its leaders, which indicate recognition of what this book is about. Were that the case there would be strength and reality enough. I am not impugning anyone's commitment here, for the long dedication of many is indeed impressive. What I am impugning is the model of ordained ministry and so of church and theology and spirituality which go with it. They may have served well in their time, but they now need to be rediscovered in other forms.

In 1984 I had a sabbatical period at Heythrop College in London which gave me immense help in looking again at ministry (and at much else besides) after years of experience and at a depth that, good though it was, my initial training never penetrated to. This book is a direct result of that work there and I deliberately offer it for debate in the church. To me at least the work has been truly a revelation, that is, one bringing what seems an undeniably authentic perspective and focus to the present critical time. I would like to express my warmest gratitude to the staff of Heythrop and to Joseph Laishley, Head of Christian Doctrine.

Finally, there is a way in which things are often dismissed as being 'merely academic'. This expression seems to me to be a twofold indictment: of people who thus can just write off the wealth of wisdom in academies as being out of touch with ordinary experience; and of that persistent dualism I shall be dealing with throughout this book. However, if to the reader who has got even so far this book seems 'too academic', let me assure him or her in words of Harry Williams which later I shall quote more precisely: true theology, like the work of the poet or the dramatist, is written in blood. This book, believe me, is by no means written in mere ideas and ink but is certainly written in blood.

CHAPTER ONE

A Time of Change

There is a story of a South American explorer who captured a chameleon and brought it back to civilization, where it became the life and soul of parties. It would be put upon ladies' dresses and watched as it changed to the appropriate colour. All went marvellously well until, alas, an invitation to Scotland, where the chameleon got on to a tartan kilt. So shattering was the experience that from that moment on it was a mixed-up chameleon, never quite knowing who it was or what it was to be, disintegrated by legion spirits.

Many people today in our society, and indeed throughout the world, have also been experiencing very great confusion. Those who are older cannot recognize the world they once knew so well. So many familiar landmarks have disappeared. Where are the stable features of life which once seemed so assured: the authority of government, of law and order, of parents, school and church? Where is the morality which once was so generally respected? Where is discipline? Where is the religion backing those things up? There is an uncertainty and a casualness in contrast to former times. 'Doing your own thing' has become a catchphrase, as if there are no longer absolutes which are universally acknowledged. To people who ask questions like this, and indeed not just to them, behaviour seems so casual. Dress, an outward sign, has often become casual too. So has language, not merely in the form of so-called bad language, but more generally in thorough disregard for accuracy and traditional forms. New words and usages have been accepted, it seems, just as soon as they have tripped off the tongue.

Then, unlike the 'old films' now often nostalgically shown on television, modern plays and films disturbingly no longer have happy endings; indeed often they have no proper endings at all. They go through lounge and bedroom and kitchen, but say only the ordinary things of life we know so well. They still leave us with our problems and our pains; they just peter out, without giving the kind of hope that we once believed in, confronting us with 'reality', but a reality which seems altogether too immediate and too disturbing. Art seems scarcely recognizable in the old, familiar, beautiful and understandable ways. And why is music so dissonant, so disorderly?

Ours is a restless age. Car and motorway have brought huge changes making us a people apparently always on the move; aircraft and modern communications make the world a global village. And all these changes seem to relate to others beneath the surface of our lives. Everything now seems to be questioned. There is a restlessness for new experience, and if something does not readily satisfy the thirsting soul it will often be regarded as readily disposable. Like the coffee it drinks, our mobile society often seems instant, and when its failings are exposed it turns tolerantly from what is 'only human', bravely and pragmatically to 'get on with life'. Where now are the older virtues of patience, perseverance and simply being content? There seems to be a continual cry for freedom, liberation, which is not always easy to understand, which seems rather to be selfishness and lawlessness, to be suppressed by return to law and order. Marriage and family life have become weak. And finally religion, once a foundation stone of life, whether people attended church or not, seems to have changed almost out of all recognition, except perhaps in the shires. Even bishops seem to doubt truths thought to be fundamental to the faith. A new breed of clergy seems to be about, perhaps more human but often too hard to recognize – sometimes more like social workers. The old language of the service books has been rudely supplanted by a modern one. New churches often do not look like churches at all. Services often seem casual. Yes, let the children come to church; yes, get the young ones in through modern ways; yes, our faith should make us joyful; yes, there should be neighbourliness in our churches (though perhaps not physically, during worship). But for all this, those who are older will very likely say; is not something fundamental, something much deeper than what has become accepted, in danger of being lost? Indeed has it not already been lost in our confused, chameleon-like modern society and world, which shifts only from fashion to fashion, from one new thing to another, so that it seems no more than a reflection of constantly shifting images?

So our world may seem to those who are older; but confusion is by no means limited just to them, and in today's fast-changing life with a looser family structure there is a wider gap between the generations. The young are so irresponsible, the older ones may say. But they may in turn be asked, 'Was that world you made and passed on to us really any better?' Those who retort in this way will be speaking from a different standpoint; indeed one so fundamentally different that the older generation will not actually be aware of it unless they can go through a kind of conversion in the way they look at life. To put it at its simplest, the different standpoint takes people more fundamentally for their own sake, rather than in a context of values, so to speak set outside them, over against them. It is one which looks for richer experience in present life – which after all is the only one we can strictly know and from which alone all knowledge and belief about 'other' life can spring – rather than simply hoping in the present for something better in some other life, some heaven. This standpoint is one which also looks towards the world in which we live – indeed a material world – and our environment, fundamentally for its own sake, rather than treating it as a mere backcloth to our lives, and perhaps a profane one at that.

Language, if it can be accurately listened to, is always a telling indicator of what people believe they are about, and two different standpoints, in tension with each other, can surely be detected from it in our time. Some words, it is true, are common to both, but even then the emphasis is significantly different. Thus the one standpoint, the older one, speaks in terms of law, order, duty, discipline, tradition, what is right and what is wrong, what is thought out rather than what is felt, locates centres for our lives which are, so to speak, beyond, outside, other than ourselves, gives priority to the individual rather than the communal, the masculine rather than the feminine. The other standpoint, the newer one, speaks rather in terms of love, care, compassion, help, acceptance, tolerance, freedom, justice, rights, needs, what is felt and intuited rather than what is primarily reasoned and thought out, relationships, communication, family, team, group, the communal rather than the individual, the human, the here and now as the centre of our lives, the predominance of feminine over masculine. But this new standpoint is far from being fully worked out and established as yet, and in the process there is much confusion for the newer voices too.

Now if this analysis is correct, clearly there must be considerable polarization, considerable conflict in society and the world, and this will be particularly expressed between the generations. For the differences are not merely about opinions on which generations have always had to agree to differ, but much more fundamentally about life and what we believe it to be and what we believe ourselves to be. The differences, highlighted by conflict between the generations, are about the view one is to hold of human beings and their place in life, the meaning of their lives. So criticism of such things as morality and aesthetics, for example, calls for the utmost sensitivity and care and vision, because views in this area can only arise out of a vision of what man and his life are about. To speak of ideals or values over against man, to speak of God, of the commandments, of the need to be truly human – all this is ultimately, after all, a matter of speaking of human beings in one way or another. The crucial question is: what kinds of human beings are being implied? And it will not do in that case simplistically to condemn the present from the standpoint of the past, appealing though nostalgia for a golden age will always be to those faced with a disturbing present.

Again, if this analysis of two fundamentally different and polarized standpoints is correct, the search for genuine landmarks must also be undertaken with sensitivity, care and vision. In our churches, specifically, it will not do just to reinforce the tradition, be it of Bible or of church order, suspecting all else of being 'debilitating liberal theology', much as every human being must have security in something. The question perpetually begged is, of course: security in precisely what? Indeed, it should be asked whether 'security' is the proper model anyway for thinking of the foundation for human life. The person who is consumed with love for others, for instance, will scarcely ever think that way, and yet is more alive than probably anybody else. The crucial question, however, is whether we are willing to surrender our selves, our experience and our own present to someone else's experience and present in some other situation in the past – which is what 'the tradition' actually is. And if in some sense we must surrender ourselves, precisely in what way and in what sense, and at what point in our own experience? Are we only willing to surrender our selves, our own experience and our very present, admittedly in the name of God, in such a way that we gobble down the Bible like a pill or just become inured to a church which 'has always done it that way and will for ever'?

But it might also be asked: are those who fundamentally reinforce the tradition turning away from a tide in human affairs and human history in which we should be immersed because perhaps we are blind and have little understanding of and love for and patience with what happens in the world? And in our church-world have we forgotten what it really is simply and ordinarily to live? Have we lost sight of the fact, in our essentially two-world mentality, that Bible and church were originally born in and properly speak of just one world, this one that we know now, and that while there will be points of separation, we ought not to, and indeed cannot, separate ourselves from human affairs and human history? To try to do so, perhaps referring to God's judgment upon the world (for which we can, of course, find support in many biblical texts), is actually to create a wrong division, if division of one world and one history is the right way of thinking anyway. It sets up a wrong relationship between the church and the world which the church then has to wrestle with, in so doing making illegitimate demands on all its resources, material and personal, until it turns into bones so dry that they cannot be made to live again without fresh spirit, which must be in the context of the world in one way or another.

There are clear precedents in Christian history of times when the tide that is running today, despite the two-sided nature of any simply human movement, flowed well enough with Christian understanding and so released new vitality, inspiring new theology precisely of the incarnational kind being produced by contemporary modern theologians – one might think of Karl Rahner on the Catholic side and Jürgen Moltmann on the Protestant – bringing renewed understanding of the church's pastoral relationship of the world, its mission and its own life in every part.

The greatest influence on this tide in our piece of human history or, to spell it out for what it is, this humanizing revolution, has been the growing authority of science, obviously traceable back to the seventeenth century but gathering strength after the Second World War.

Most of us in Western societies will be aware of mighty achievements, through scientific know-how. Space exploration, computers, the silicon chip, new skills in medicine and in healing injuries of the mind – all such scientific and technological achievements are obvious. Less obvious has been the influence of science upon other areas of life. In philosophy, traditional idealism has been collapsing in the face of empiricism and logical positivism. Now existentialism holds sway in many places. What we can claim to know as human beings is pinned down to what we find within human experience. In art, in its different forms of painting, sculpture, architecture, literature, music and so on emphasis has shifted from portraying realities 'beyond' human eye and ear and mind to those 'within experience'. Religion and morality have also undergone similar massive change to become, so to speak, more earth-centred. The thinking of three figures in particular, Darwin, Marx and Freud, has had a huge influence on the way we now see ourselves, as people determined by evolutionary, social and psychological forces, largely beyond our control. Their thinking was, of course, based on scientific method.

While this development in thinking provides penetrating insights into human nature and society, it has also contributed to an undermining of personal responsibility: on the one hand, through naive optimism and easy-going liberalism, now clearly shattered by the way our recent history has gone; on the other, through a belief that we cannot help the way we are and cannot be otherwise. Parents in particular will have experienced the sometimes devastating extent of their children's questioning, questioning which they themselves were not competent to answer. Sometimes the entire foundation of their lives has come under scrutiny. Why shouldn't I behave in this way? Why should I do that? How do you know that God exists? How do you know that there is life after death? Hasn't science disproved the Bible?

All this fundamental change did not leave theology untouched. In 1963 a little book by the then Bishop of Woolwich, John Robinson, called *Honest to God*, signalled similar changes in the theology of the church. Under the influence of the same scientific and humanizing spirit, traditional ways of thinking about God as being up there and out there were 'demythologized'. Since we live in a world quite different from that of the Bible and the West before Galileo, new ways of speaking of God had now to be found. Indeed God had, so to speak, to be relocated. The direction and focus of our experience of God are, it was claimed, rather different, and this is far more than a matter of mere language. God is now to be seen as 'down here' where we are, in the world, in the depths of human experience, as the Ground underlying all things, as the ultimate Reality of all the realities that we experience. Some saw a danger here of reducing God to being merely another dimension of the ordinary things of life, as in a sense being not significantly different from them. John Robinson had to answer the charge that this new thinking was no more than pantheism, i.e. that God was no more than the energy most people discern in things and that to worship this God would be mere nature-worship. However, *Honest to God* reflected the selfsame movement affecting the whole of life over this time. The centres of attention had now become the world and human experience in it. Man had now become the measure of all things. And Robinson's theology was echoed strongly elsewhere. In the very year *Honest to God* appeared, a book of prayers was published, again with a massive appeal: *Prayers of Life*, by Michel Quoist. Here certainly God was still 'up there', for to see life truly we had to 'rise high'. But the overall emphasis was on God's being found down in ordinary life: at the football match, in the underground, in the brick, in my friend, and so on. Many found this vision of prayer very refreshing, releasing them out of churchiness into the world. In this book the meditations were appropriately on human experience and the experience of Jesus the man.

But all this produced a crisis in the 1970s for ordinands in theological colleges and for clergymen in parishes simply over the way one should pray. For some, prayer could no longer be a matter of first 'going aside' and then entering life in that spirit of prayer; it was now a matter of simply entering life like any other human being to discover God already there. Life was prayer. In his *Honest to God* Robinson took up Dietrich Bonhoeffer's description of humanity having 'come of age'. What was being said here was that modern man, through the scientific know-how now given him, was liberated from earlier childish dependent attitudes towards God and life and was to stand on his own two feet. Indeed, in new forms of worship he was invited to do just that, rather than kneel. He could, of course, stand on his own feet if he was sure of his 'ground'. And now, having 'come of age', he should take on larger responsibility both for his own life and for the life of the world. Appropriately, the gospel was often described as a 'social gospel'. God was to be discovered particularly in serving the sick and the hungry, the naked and those in prison, and so on. The parable of the sheep and the goats in Matthew 25 became a central biblical text. According to the title of a subsequent book by Robinson, God was said to have a human face.[1] Out of all the gospel events, emphasis centred on the incarnation, on Jesus the man. Here, it was being said, by himself taking flesh God had affirmed all humanity, raising it to a completely new value, and by doing so in the poor and anonymous Jesus of Nazareth he had specifically put himself with the poor. With a growing awareness of the poor and powerless of the world and of the inner city the emphasis seemed particularly appropriate. But it is clear that this massive change in theological thinking has scarcely been reflected in every part of the church.

It is indeed obvious! But to be fair, there is a duality in Christian theology which accounts for much of this fact: a duality-within-unity, so to speak, or, to put it another way, a tension between polarities within which we all have to live. On the one hand there are realities 'beyond' or 'other than' the realities of the world and ordinary life, traditionally identified with the holy; on the other there are realities 'within', 'deep down' in the world, the ordinary, 'the here and now' and indeed the secular, which are equally holy. To use other language, which again is quite inadequate and only points the way, there is the duality of the transcendent and the immanent, of the 'journey outwards' and the 'journey inwards', of the 'upwards' and the 'downwards' – but the character of all these polarized realities is such that they can all be only ultimately one and the same reality.

All human beings, and not just Christians, are given with their very existence a continuing living in tension. The tension points to, and indeed is, the reality and mystery of God verbalized, for instance – and still most inadequately – in the Christian doctrine of the Trinity. But we human beings ordinarily find the living in tension far too much for us. Yeats actually prophesied the reversal of Christian values:

> Things fall apart; the centre cannot hold;
> Mere anarchy is loosed upon the world,
> The blood-dimmed tide is loosed and everywhere
> The ceremony of innocence is drowned.[2]

Almost inevitably, then, we get drawn towards graven images of one kind or another. Because we want security, and choose that rather than living openly towards mystery, we take the forms and shapes and shadows for reality and live to those instead. We idolize the shapes of other people's experience of and grappling for the mystery of God in the forms of Bible and church tradition and try to make them God. Similarly we idolize humanity, so that the fundamental challenge of the gospel which actually 'reaches down to joints and marrow', as Hebrews 4.12f. puts it, becomes domesticated and tamed and, particularly in modern times, little more than dressed-up humanism. There is again, then, a duality-within-unity, a tension between polarities, within which we have to live as a given fact of our existence – but which often proves too much for our stunted imagination and limited vision. What can often be found then, sadly and ironically, are church people and clergy looking down their noses at those 'liberals' who, they think, have sold out to the world, and conversely others looking scornfully at those 'conservatives' imprisoned in their irrelevant cultic world. All idols must finally fall apart in our very hands, and the church, under the selfsame conditions as everything else, has to live within the tension of duality-within-unity, and in no way can escape it. It will experience the tension, too, in particular ways and with particular emphases at different points in its own and in human history. And since, as we have seen, the experience of any group or institution becomes most acute in its leadership, it will be the church's priesthood or ordained ministry which will experience the tension and reveal its concrete effects most of all. Priesthood or the ordained ministry stands right at the intersection, so to speak, of on the one hand realities beyond or other than the ordinary and the secular and, on the other, realities within or deep down those very things. It is therefore inevitably stretched this way and that within itself, within the church – hence the continuing disunity of the churches, ultimately for this reason and nothing else – and within the particular character of periods in Christian and human history.

So it is, then, that struggles for identity and truth and purpose continually emerge between priesthood or ordained ministry and laity, between 'priests' and 'ministers', between 'high' and 'low', between those for church renewal from within the church and those for church renewal from the world, and so on. But in that case what should be a true reading of the signs of our own uncertain and changing time, and a proper response to it?

The purpose of this book is to draw out this very tension, this duality-within-unity, as focussed in the church and most acutely in the priesthood or the ordained ministry, through a comparison of three theologies at different times since the turn of this century. On the strength of that comparison and the kind of analysis already indicated in this chapter, a way will be pointed forward out of not only a time of undoubted uncertainty but also an undeniable crisis for the church as a whole and particularly, as one would naturally expect, for priesthood or the ordained ministry for which, as we shall see in the next chapter, there are so many critical problems. It seems clear that, valuable

as the traditional model of priesthood or the ordained ministry
has been for church and world over many centuries, it is now in
virtual collapse. By the same token, that model and image of the
church is also in collapse. Like it or not, priesthood or the
ordained ministry and the traditional model of the church are
coming, apparently inevitably, to a historic point of major
reformation.

CHAPTER TWO

Recent Problems

Crisis of numbers

Anyone who reads surveys and statistics about ministry in our Western countries at all carefully will note an apparent contradiction. On the one hand numerous declarations indicate satisfaction about the ministry (even public opinion is much more positive towards clergy than, for example, towards politicians); on the other hand we find countless frustrations and restrictions, and sometimes desperate fatalism. There is a very great deal of good will and idealism and almost as much disillusionment. Perhaps this is a general human phenomenon . . . However . . . the ministry is at the moment in one of those rare historical stages of transition and reconstruction. It cannot go any further as it is now, either here in Holland or – with a number of exceptions – elsewhere.[1]

So spoke Jan Kerkofs, a Belgian Jesuit and Secretary General of *Pro Mundi Vita*, a well-known Catholic international study and documentation centre gathering facts and statistics relating to church affairs from all over the world. He was addressing a conference of students and lecturers from the Dutch and Belgian theological seminaries. The main reason he gave for his forecast was sheer lack of numbers. The figures he quoted, crude though he claimed them to be, and somewhat dated though they now are, made his case overwhelmingly. Whether in South Africa or the Philippines, Spain or North America, he painted a picture of declining numbers of candidates for ordination, and an increasing average age of the clergy, to such a degree that already many communities had no resident priest at all. Even in Third World countries where there was some increase in ordinations, this increase in no way kept pace with the rise in population. With the significant exceptions of Poland[2] and Yugoslavia, the number of those leaving the ministry or dying was vastly higher than the number ordained. Britain was a fortunate exception, with the replacement of almost 75% of clergy dying, resigning or retiring; but in Italy the figure was 50%, in Germany 34%, in France 18% and in Holland under 8%.

In almost all countries throughout the world the shortage of priests is growing at a terrifying rate. Because they alone are authorized to administer the sacraments, and in particular to preside at the eucharist, this means that an increasing number of Catholic communities are being cut off from their source of life. And as this goes on year after year, the situation gets steadily worse and the chances of its being remedied in traditional terms get less and less.

Nor is the crisis of numbers in the priesthood or ordained ministry confined to the Catholic church; it is being experienced equally in the Church of England and the Free Churches. In September 1983 a crucial document with precisely the same concern, *A Strategy for the Church's Ministry*, was published by the Church Information Office for the Church of England. Its author was John Tiller, Chief Secretary to the Advisory Council for the Church's Ministry, a central body acting for the bishops, directly related to the selection for training of those claiming to be called to the ordained ministry, which generally monitors the condition of the ministry. In this position, not unlike that of Jan Kerkhofs, Tiller was able to observe trends in Anglican church life much resembling those in Catholicism. His strategy was directed towards a hope expressed in November 1980 that General Synod, 'while getting to grips with the now urgent practical issues, will seek an opportunity to take a longer-term and more speculative view of the way in which ministry may need to be exercised, not perhaps immediately but within the lifetime of younger members of the present Synod and of young men and women now offering themselves, and being trained, for ministry' (*Strategy*, p. 4) and towards a need identified by Synod, following the rejection by the Church of England in 1982 of a new relationship of growth towards visible unity with non-conformist churches, for an agreed theology of ministry and priesthood. That rejection, like similar ones before it, had been brought about not least from those in the Church of England who were concerned for a 'catholic' priesthood and all else that went with it. The strategy also represented one more effort in a succession of efforts, going back at least to 1963, to think radically about the ordained ministry in difficult situations.

1963 had seen the publication by the Church Information Office of another report on *The Deployment and Payment of the Clergy*, produced by Leslie Paul. Faced with loss of membership, a decline in the church's influence, and the location of most of the clergy in the country while most people were living in towns and cities, along with a potential declining ratio of clergy to population (through a population explosion which he forecast but which actually never came), Paul foresaw a critical point ahead for the viability of ordained ministry, though he thought its coming would be slow. His analysis was based on the number of full-time clergy in the dioceses in 1961, 15,488, and the fact that for several years the annual rate of ordinations, while in fact exceeding 600, had been greater than annual losses. To fill the gap, he pointed to the need for more ordinations, supplemented by the development of lay and non-stipendiary ministries. A further report published in 1967, *Partners in Ministry*, took Paul's proposals further.

However, by the mid-1970s, with numbers of clergy diminishing even more, the very future of the ordained ministry had become very doubtful, and deployment had become more a matter of fair shares of what was available to keep the institution going. The number recommended for training for ordination to stipendiary ministry fell between 1965 and 1976 from 348 to 254. A minimum number of 11,600 full-time clergy was recognized as necessary in 1986 if traditional parochial structures were to continue to be viable. Some dioceses, especially rural ones, foresaw the end of the traditional pattern of ministry with every parish having its own priest or minister. Some expected to stretch resources, and clergy in particular,

even further by creating yet larger parishes. Some would cut back
the specialist ministries which had imaginatively been developed as changes in society's life and the church's tasks had
been acknowledged, so as to have clergy to maintain the
traditional parochial pattern. Some began thinking about re-
cruiting non-stipendiary clergy and an ordained ministry produced locally in some way. Then in 1976 General Synod endorsed
a proposal from the bishops for an annual target of 400 to 500
recommendations for full-time ministry. Recommendations
actually increased from 349 to 404 in 1980, but in 1981 they fell to
361 and in 1982 to 350, while ordinations themselves remained
virtually static between 1977 to 1982, varying only from 301 to
313. The bishops' target, then, was reached in one year only.
Indeed, from the latest statistics from the Advisory Council
itself, although numbers put forward for possible recommenda-
tion seem now to be on the increase – dramatically in 1985, at 347
by nearly 10% over the previous year – actual recommendations
for full-time ministry numbered 303 in 1983 and 306 in 1984.
Whatever other interpretations of these trends are to be made,
one undeniably could be that there is now something unattractive about the image and model of priesthood or ordained
ministry. (And here it is perhaps significant that such increase as
there has been in the latest period seems largely accounted for by
growing numbers of women putting themselves forward and
being recommended.)

Furthermore, since 1963 the nation's population has increased by approximately four million, while the number of
full-time clergy has declined from 15,488 in 1962 to 10,789 in
1982, and a large proportion of these are near retirement, having
entered the ordained ministry after the Second World War.
'There is clearly little possibility that the minimum 11,600
full-time priests will become available to staff the parochial
system.'[3] On the other hand, paralleling some Catholic experience, Tiller also notes that, following decline in church membership as a whole since 1960 and especially a trough in the
mid-1970s, between 1976 and 1980 there were signs of 'modest
recovery'. 'It is particularly interesting that such growth as
there has been has taken place at precisely the time when
numbers of parochial clergy have become dangerously low . . . I

think that most people who have been closely in touch over the last twenty years would have little doubt about the real reason for recent church growth at a time of clergy decline: it has been a period during which the clergy have become a much smaller part of the church's total ministry' (*Strategy*, p. 22). Is it perhaps again, then, that it is the image and model of priesthood or ordained ministry which pose the problem, rather than, say, simply the waywardness of the world in our time? Is it perhaps that the image and model of priesthood or ordained ministry (and indeed all that goes with them) have served well enough in their own time, but are now unattractive and in fact against the tide currently running in our piece of human history?

With the growing shortage of priests, two other issues have immediately been thrown up, and they in their own ways take us to the self-same heart of our understanding of priesthood or ordained ministry, and in turn of our understanding of the church and ultimately of theology itself.

The ordination of women

One issue for the Church of England, though not for it alone, is the ordination of women. If women are claiming to be called to priesthood, why not recognize them and ordain them and go some way towards solving the problem of numbers? That is one argument that can be heard today. Within the worldwide Anglican Communion other churches have done just this, Hong Kong for forty years. It is also argued that if deaconesses and women parish workers are already exercising a full ministry and even leading churches, there is no reason why they should not also be enabled to celebrate the eucharist and give absolution, as the natural completion of what they already do. Where is the common sense, let alone theological sense, it is asked, in a woman being engaged daily in deep and authoritative ministry with people and yet having to wait with her congregation for a vicar to come to say words of consecration and absolution so that the service can be valid, particularly when he has to be wheeled up at some distance from elsewhere? Where is the common sense, let alone theological sense, in a woman hearing the outpourings of a guilty heart and by the very nature of her

presence actualizing Christ's forgiveness and reconciliation,
and then having to send the penitent to a priest, to confess again
from cold, if the form of sacramental confession is needed?
These are grass-roots questions. And indeed the Church of
England actually stated in its 1983 General Synod that there can
be no theological objection to women priests, though in
deference to both Anglo-Catholics within its membership and
relations with the Roman Catholic Church it was also stated
that the time was not yet ripe. Since then, in fact, looking
towards unity with the Roman Catholic Church, and beyond
that even with the Eastern Churches, who have said that unity
would be unthinkable were women to be ordained priests,
Anglo-Catholics have worked to reinforce their position against
that statement and have actually strengthened their hand in
elections to key positions in the Synod. For them the ordination
of women can never be right. For, they say, Christ himself chose
men as his apostles and they subsequently chose men as their
successors, and in every succeeding generation to the present
day, unbroken in continuity, the church – the true church, that
is – has equally and deliberately chosen men throughout the
entire threefold ministry of bishops, priests and deacons which
is, so they say, the very heart of its life.

For all that, it could equally be said that Christ also chose
Jews, yet priesthood obviously moved subsequently to Gentiles.
The counter-argument then is that the male priesthood was not
and never has been historically or culturally created or conditioned. It is above and other than such things. The priesthood
which, it is said, Christ gave when, again it is said, he founded
his church, is in fact 'ontological': by that it is meant that it 'is',
eternally and unchanging, that it is something essential and
fundamental. And the nature of this priesthood (and all that
goes along with it) is ontologically 'other than' the ordinary and
simply human, so that it is most naturally embodied in
maleness, the natural inclination of which is to point away from
the ordinary and the earthly, as opposed to femaleness, the
natural inclination of which is to embrace it and to be embodied
in it and to point down to the depths. Many major assumptions
are made on both sides of the argument here which will be
teased out and examined in the following chapters. At this

point, however, we simply need to see that the question of the ordination of women is not an isolated issue to be considered on its own but, with the crisis of numbers which I have already mentioned and subsequent issues to be considered in this chapter, actually goes to the very heart of the image and model we have of priesthood or ordained ministry and indeed of our understanding of church and the whole of theology.

Celibacy

The other immediate question raised urgently for the Catholic Church is why priesthood is reserved for celibate men? To quote Jan Kerkhofs again: 'Over the last fifteen years tens of thousands of priests have resigned from the ministry. In most cases the reason they gave was enforced celibacy. In many areas groups of married priests once again want to take an active part in pastoral ministry . . . In the Diocesan Conference of priests in Barcelona in 1977 – in which 535 priests took part – the following resolutions were passed: to ordain married men in specific circumstances and for pastoral reasons; to open up again to married priests all offices which can be filled by laity; to ordain women to the diaconate; to allow optional celibacy to diocesan priests.'[4] Kerkhofs also cited an impressive list of other bodies who support this kind of change. And the argument for relaxation of the rule of celibacy, he reminds us, is not merely one of numbers, but of the suffering of living people: the tragedies of the priest who marries while claiming a genuine vocation to priesthood, who then comes to be regarded as a traitor – Pope Paul VI used the word 'Judas'; of the young man wanting to be married and to serve the church as a pastor but (reminding us of how precisely the issue of the ordination of women becomes focussed) will be allowed to do anything except preside at the eucharist and forgive sins; of believers who cannot have a pastor even though candidates exist, or who have to keep on an incompetent pastor because he is a celibate priest; or church leaders themselves torn between their episcopal responsibility towards the grass roots and loyalty to the Holy See.

In the Eastern Church married men may be ordained, though

not as bishops. In the West, however, male celibacy is held by Roman Catholics as essential to the nature of priesthood, though not long ago Cardinal Hume was reported as saying in public in Britain that the time might come when married men would actually be ordained priests.

And if that happened, what in fact would be lost? Some pastoral availability, it might be said, but this response already carries with it assumptions about priesthood or ordained ministry which need to be examined. For instance, what is 'availability' understood to be for? What kind of priesthood or ordained ministry is it that is so 'pastorally available'? Questions like this again go to the very heart of our image and model of priesthood or ordained ministry, of church and theology. What might, or rather would, be lost were celibacy to be relaxed is what is often called the 'mystical'; that is, a spirit and a character which is essentially other than the ordinary and the simply human. This mystical element, it is claimed, is the essential and ontological nature of the priesthood. The claim is, as we have seen, that it is this that has been passed down from Christ himself in unbroken historical succession, generation after generation (though modern New Testament scholarship has pointed out that members of the Twelve, like Peter, actually had wives). This mystical element is thought to be appropriately and ontologically embodied in a priesthood which is male as well as being celibate, an argument that we have also seen brought up in connection with the ordination of women.

But the assumptions made are open to criticism. For one thing, modern psychology would readily criticize the simple dichotomy between male and female and see both characteristics in both men and women. Again, we shall tease out and examine other assumptions in the following chapters. For the moment, as before, let us simply note once again at this point that on the one hand there is the argument against celibacy from the grass roots, on grounds of humanity and practicality, and on the other the argument from the 'ontological', that which is beyond and above all those things, that which is other than the ordinary and the human. From this latter standpoint it is argued that, so far as marriage and sexuality are concerned, celibacy not only can transfigure human energies for love in the beyond but also point up the universal truth that even the richest experience of marriage and sexuality is only for a time and must actually look beyond – a perspective from which modern society, so obsessed by sex, would do well to learn. Here is a truth which certainly ought to be recognized, but we can do that in different ways.

Like the issue of the ordination of women, this issue of a celibate male priesthood is not an isolated one to be considered on its own but takes us, like that and yet others to follow, to the very heart of our image and model of priesthood or ordained ministry, church and theology. That the Church of England's own crisis in numbers can in no way be a result of enforced celibacy surely confirms that. Here certainly is a challenge to priesthood and all else which is much more fundamental and, as we shall go on to see, set in an even wider context.

Crisis of identity

Certainly in Western cultures, and in Third World countries too, a considerable change has been taking place. Indeed, significantly for Western cultures, the change in Third World countries has often in fact represented an overturning of the traditions originally brought from them through colonization and accompanying Christian mission in favour of an indigenous humanization from the grass roots. Where this new voice has actually been heard in Western cultures, then – for instance in recognition of the institutionalized injustice between trading nations and the crisis of world hunger, and in the growing interest in liberation theology – the humanizing revolution already under way has been reinforced. This humanizing revolution in terms of one world has been inspired, largely unconsciously, by the poor.

One aspect of the humanizing change among Anglican clergy in the West, and in England in particular, has been traced by Anthony Russell in his important book *The Clerical Profession*[5]: the historical and sociological changes through the nineteenth and twentieth centuries have left the clergyman, in a highly professionalized society, stripped of his traditional roles like those of provider of education and almsgiver, and now not altogether knowing what he is for. Is his distinctiveness now only in taking services, which laity themselves are now also proving themselves competent to lead? Is it just in the gaps that our more professionalized society cannot and will not cover, much like the voluntary workers whose help the government particularly looks to encourage? Is he a kind of clergy of the gaps, much like an earlier God of the gaps? Or does his distinctiveness lie in the fact that he does what others do but on another level, in some different quality of life? Where the answer has been in the direction of the first of these three possibilities, we have seen distinctiveness emphasized in various ways, but often at the cost of even greater and more disastrous separation from the world at large (disastrous for both church and world). Where it has been in the direction of the second and often perhaps of the third possibility as well, we have seen the throwing off of the strong church-orientated life of the past as being no longer relevant. In the former, clergy have often welcomed the stripping away of traditional roles, for, they have said, they have now been freed to centre more completely upon God, their essential calling. And indeed there is a huge truth here which any priest or minister ought to know. But on the other hand an equally huge question is simply being begged: what kind of God, what kind of theology, is being implied? Clearly it is the God and the theology centred on the 'beyond', that which is 'other than' the ordinary and the human, that which is in separation. Is the world not also the very stuff of God and of theology?

So other clergy, on the contrary, have felt this to be simply shutting God up in the sanctuary. In the latter kind of response to the three questions I mentioned earlier, clergy have then sought to discover or display their distinctiveness by simply being alongside other human beings in everyday life, taking off their clerical collars and pursuing a call as 'worker priests'. But here, too, the same question as before is simply being begged: what kind of God, what kind of theology, is being implied? Is this not merely a dressed-up humanism, and perhaps scarcely even that? Is it not merely a capitulation to modern secularism, with all the dangerous potential of that (again for both church and world)? In the midst of all this polarization, many have been

left in limbo. According to Russell, the clergyman's profession
is still largely frozen in nineteenth-century attitudes and
expectations, both within the church and without, with enormous consequences for modern times. A comparison of the tone
of the ten-yearly Lambeth conferences through this century can
be seen to reflect a good deal of this. In 1978 a report entitled
'What is the Church for?' took quite a new tone in speaking of
'bewilderment', 'our own sinfulness', 'uncertainty about what
our responses should be' amid 'the complexities and turbulence
of our societies and of the world at large.'[6]

And we must remember that the confusion is not merely an
academic or a so-called ecclesiastical one; it has the utmost
bearing upon real people. Churchpeople as a whole have, of
course, been experiencing this confusion, but the clergy have
been experiencing it most – and their wives and families if they
have them. These have been at the very intersection of so
many different stresses pulling this way and that, some of
course in the very nature of the continuing and necessary
theological tension in which they are caught – of the 'beyond'
with the 'within' so to speak. However, many more stresses
come from the countless false attitudes and expectations to
which Russell himself points, springing from a fundamental
lack of understanding of what has been going on in our own
piece of human history and what that means for the image and
model of priesthood or ordained ministry and so indeed for
church and theology as a whole. It will have been those most
concerned for a living image and model consonant with the
new realities of modern times rather than one fossilized in
some fantasy church-world, and who have been concerned to
engage rather than disengage, who will have carried within
themselves these stresses most, with perhaps important consequences for health and married life. Indeed, it has surely been
for this reason, the need for a genuinely living image and
model, that many recent ordinands from training colleges have
been found insisting more upon their 'rights' and caring more
for their own dignity as persons, in a way that older priests will
misinterpret as an unwillingness for the sacrifices that *they*
were brought up to. And in words of Victor de Waal from a
collection of essays about the ordained ministry actually given

to me and my contemporaries in 1969, when we were about to
be ordained: 'For many who are in positions of isolation, the
old clerical piety, which accepted loneliness as part of the
priestly vocation, no longer consoles. For theirs is not the
loneliness of the pioneer apostle, but the isolation of those who
sense they are being squeezed out of society which, in according them the title of "reverend", includes them in the same
category as other antique and picturesque functionaries left
over from a former age.'[7] The solution to this crucial problem
of identity and to all that must follow from it for both church
and theology as a whole is to be found, as both Russell and de
Waal, along with many others, believe, in the rediscovery of
the priest's or ordained minister's place within the community; with the church rediscovered as a community and
indeed even beyond that, in the community of the world at
large. We shall see more of this in due course. Again in de
Waal's words: 'The ordained ministry is likely to rediscover its
nature and functions only in so far as the church comes to
terms with itself again as a voluntary association, and is
prepared to live more of its life at the level of groups where its
members can really meet, know and help one another, and so
together serve Christ in the world. The signs that this has in
fact already been happening for some time are not far to seek.'
And yet again, this time quoting Karl Rahner as he spoke in
1965 about the church of the future: 'We are all one in Christ,
the ultimate difference is the degree of love, for God and the
brothers; distinctions of office are necessary but entirely secondary and provisional, a burden, a service, a sacred responsibility . . . The bishop will not look very different from any other
official in a small voluntary group effectively dependent on the
good will of that group . . . It will be clear and plain to see, that
all dignity and office in the church is uncovenanted service,
carrying with it no honour in the world's eyes . . . perhaps it
will no longer constitute a profession in the social and secular
sense at all.' These are words of perhaps the most influential
and most respected Catholic theologian of our time. They go to
the very heart of our images and models of priesthood or
ordained ministry and of church and, in the end, to the very
heart of theology as a whole.

Grass-roots communities

And the context of the problem of numbers becomes even wider. For a major phenomenon of our piece of history has been the mushrooming of communities, both secular and religious, in both Western societies and the Third World, as a grass-roots response to the thirst for the rediscovery of the personal in a harsh and anonymous world. The dream of community can be seen in almost every area of life we care to look at in our time, from the small cell or house group, through anonymous housing estates and ethnic groups suddenly declared to be 'community', finally to one world. In a sense it could be misleading to use the word 'religious' to describe the very 'basic' grass-roots communities (as they are often called, particularly in the Third World) for they are actually quite different in character and centre from the traditional religious communities which have largely been passed by in this massive new movement of our time. The traditional religious communities have been experiencing a crisis of identity and purpose even more acute than that for clergy, and they are of course a step further from the world. For the basic communities, on the other hand, 'religious' significantly means living by faith reborn at the grass roots, in the world, and particularly living by faith in community. In the West the direction has been towards richer experience of community; in the Third World the concern has been with liberation from oppression and injustice caused by unjust structures of power.

So in Britain we have seen the house church movement, often ecumenical and sitting lightly to traditional institutions and their authority, appealing to the Bible, the traditional source of reformation, and to a common life of prayer and fellowship. In Britain, too, and by no means incidentally, the Church of England with its crisis of numbers in the ordained ministry has seen the development of the phenomenon of small congregations thrown back on their own resources. As yet this phenomenon has been largely papered over by pluralities of living in the country and the teaming of ministries in towns and cities, because of assumptions about priesthood or the ordained ministry which the church is wedded to and has not yet been

forced to re-examine. But certainly these have great potential for
the rediscovery of the church as Christian community.

On the world-wide scene, the Catholic church has seen many
'basic communities' emerging, groups of Christians similarly
longing for richer experience of community, particularly where
often there is no priest, but also in the Third World, where the
motive force is liberation from injustices which cause deprivation of such basic necessities as food and proper housing. In all
such communities or potentials for community, the language,
significantly, is about person and community and human
dignity, for the basis of their life is a renewed vision of humanness
'in Christ'. But the problems which they all pose take us again
right to the very heart of our image and model of priesthood or
ordained ministry, of what we understand the church to be and,
in the end, to our image of theology as a whole. Though the
Catholic basic communities are gathered in the name of Jesus,
pray and read the Bible together, share and experience community together, and actively pursue Christian mission in their
locality in the Third World, usually in terms of justice, and
'witness' even to the point of giving their lives (the supreme mark
of the disciple in the early church), according to traditional
Christian understanding they cannot be recognized as fully or
even perhaps as truly Christian; they cannot celebrate the
eucharist, the wellspring of life, and therefore cannot be fully in
communion with the remainder of the 'official' church because
they have no priest. But it is vital for us to recognize that the priest
whom they lack is someone who originally would have been
taken out of the local Christian community and context in which
he experienced his calling, to be detached from ordinary life for
training in things 'other', then sent back to minister to people, it
was hoped with the right language. But minister in what
direction? The direction has surely been 'beyond', a direction
largely opposite to that inspiring these basic communities.
Traditional training has been largely for building up faith and so
helping people to bear the situation patiently, but what these
basic communities want is actual change.

Now the way I have described this contrast is deliberate, and
the priesthood or ordained ministry is a service in which I was
trained; in which I have lived and worked for years; and for which

I have the utmost respect. But it is about detachment, separation from the ordinary. It is based on that common human experience that what we yearn for at the core of our being, in heart and soul, has not been and cannot be found in ordinary life; and so, if it is to be found anywhere, it can only be found 'beyond' it, 'above' it, 'outside' it and 'apart from' it. This does not have to carry us over into the belief that the ordinary is not just ordinary but in its very nature fundamentally tainted, 'fallen', and that every human endeavour is therefore doomed to disaster from the first, for it is open to us to live in ordinary life with a sense both of 'fallenness' and of God, held in tension, in such a way that we enter life more fully still, at a deeper level and try to carry it forward to what deep down all of it longs for. But the fact about the church is that it normally does carry over this approach into the view that the world is fundamentally tainted – I suppose, because of the force of the tradition of separation and of the institutional structure of the church, because of the need of church members to keep alive their own sense of being alive, and the fact that the church does not really listen to and hear the deep longings of the human heart in ordinary life. The effect is a theological outlook which says that we can never properly begin from the human but only from the separated state, to which first we must be converted.

It is precisely this outlook which underlies the present Pope's strong opposition to priests holding office in the Nicaraguan government and to Catholic theologians like Küng, who has had his licence to teach at Catholic universities withdrawn, and Schillebeeckx and Leonardo Boff, both of whom have been under investigation. The official Catholic theological outlook is, as we have seen, wholly on the Polish model, which identifies atheism with Marxism and which because of its background has a marked feeling of being 'apart'. But since all this is the case, how can this outlook ultimately get to the heart of issues like justice and liberation as the basic communities see them? How can this traditional priesthood do other than counsel faith, looking beyond, hope in some better world 'fundamentally other' than this one? Ultimately this priesthood or ordained ministry indeed looks in 'another' direction no matter what it actually says, at worst in quite the opposite direction to what is deep down at the grass roots, and at best significantly off-set from it. And the truth is precisely the same with the similar examples in Britain and the Church of England. It also lies at the heart of all issues relating to ecumenicity. The image and model of priesthood or ordained ministry, of what we understand theology to be and ultimately of theology as a whole, is indeed the heart of the matter. So the development in the Third World of the whole new body of liberation theology and of the basic communities from which it arises is, I believe, of the utmost significance for our time, in the West as well. It is being said that the very assumptions of the Western theological tradition, originally brought to Third World countries through colonization and Christian mission, need to be broken open, no less. And when that happens, the way will be opened up for a fundamental rebirth of theology and church and priesthood or ordained ministry, worldwide and ecumenical, based on a recovery of an understanding of how theology should be done, not in separation, but from within concrete grass-root situations, and how it should be lived out in a fundamentally human way.

Tiller's concern in his strategy is ultimately to open up the church to the laity in a ministry which is fully shared. Stated so baldly, this has led many people to dismiss his approach for being 'low church', 'weak' theology or unfaithful to the tradition. Kerkhofs points to the 'majority opinion of believers and theologians, shared by most priests – where these are consulted – and by an indeterminate number of church leaders. These believe that the form of the ministry is relative; that the community of Christian believers can have great flexibility and can sometimes make far-reaching changes, like the ordination of married men; and that there can be new pastoral and priestly integration of married priests. They look for an opening up of the ministry to women; the reorganization of the whole pastoral ministry on every level in teams; and above all the 'calling' of adult church leaders and pastors by local communities instead of their 'imposition' on communities from above.'[8] All the problems cited in this chapter, as we have already seen, are in no way isolated problems to be considered on their own. As I have continually stressed, all go to the very heart of priesthood or ordained ministry, the church and theology, and together with great force raise the question whether the life once within traditional understandings is not spent, great though it may have been in sustaining our ancestors. Together all these problems exert huge pressure towards asking whether new understandings, new images and models are not now to be forged, which will draw life from and be more properly in the flow of the tide running in human affairs and our own piece of human history. Such a new endeavour would respect received tradition; indeed, how can we escape it, being the people we are? But it would not simply swallow this tradition down like a pill. What is needed is a reworking of it in our time, taking it up but then going on from it genuinely into our own present (and future), as though those whose tradition it once was, friends known and unknown, were at our side urging us on . . . and in order to find echoes and visions, intimations and inklings of their experience in our own, bringing God into focus for us in our own time. This kind of response would indeed bring about a reformation.

However, as a next stage I want to compare three theologies of priesthood and ministry in both Catholic and Anglican traditions between the turn of the century and the present time. They are the classic traditional one by R. C. Moberly, originally produced in Britain in 1897; then one by Yves Congar, wrestling in the 1950s in France, against the background of the worker-priest movement, for a full theological warrant for the ministry of the laity; and finally one by Edward Schillebeeckx from the Netherlands, precisely contemporary with the modern situation and cutting the Gordian knot so as to respond to the call from the basic communities.

First Interlude

Quite Apart from the Holy Ghost

I remember God as an eccentric millionaire,
Locked in his workshop, beard a cloud of foggy-coloured hair,
Making the stones all different, each flower and disease,
Putting the Laps in Lapland, making China for the Chinese,
Laying down the Lake of Lucerne as smooth as blue-grey lino,
Wearily inventing the appendix and the rhino.
Making the fine fur for the mink, fine women for the fur,
Man's brain a gun, his heart a bomb, his conscience – a blur.

Christ I can see much better from here,
And Christ upon the Cross is clear.
Jesus is stretched like the skin of a kite
Over the Cross, he seems in flight
Sometimes. At times it seems more true
That he is meat nailed up alive and pain all through.
But it's hard to see Christ for priests. That happens when
A poet engenders generations of advertising men.

Adrian Mitchell[1]

One night in my own home a young person became frighteningly violent in a physical way. When he calmed down he came and sat on the end of the bed in my room and began to cry. Through the crying, he said that he had been pushed around and thrown out of institution after institution since he was four years of age. As I looked at him sitting there with head bent and sobbing, I remembered a painting in one of the Passionist houses. It was a painting depicting the mockery of Christ in the hours of his suffering. The head was bent, the mocking cloak of royalty was slipping away from his shoulder, there were tears on his face and he sat on the edge of a broken pillar. It was not the physical suffering which made its impact on me and remained with me, it was the encompassing loneliness which projected itself and made an impact. As I looked at that young person that was all I could see. I mumbled sympathetically and attempted to point to a future.

An isolated and exaggerated example? Perhaps. At the same time I have looked into the eyes of too many human beings in the Inner City only to see a tragic hopelessness. There can never be an authentic philosophy of equality of opportunity unless we face up to the urgent need to admit the charade we have all been part of, as we played the game of equality itself. For me as a Christian, priest, and religious – and I know I speak for many others in this regard – the institution of Christianity has been no exception to this process of conscious or unconscious oppression. We must have done with it no matter what the price we have to pay in terms of radical renewal.

If we do so, as Christians, we do no more and no less than accept the call to denial of self to answer the call of Christ. To follow Christ means to die to oneself. To reap a new harvest, or better to work towards a future in which those who are not born will reap a new harvest, demands the death of the seed now. We are the seed living to die in an era of history, dominated by what I have called the 'contrast experience' which makes a mockery of what it is to be all that is human.

I thank God for my Faith, for my priesthood and for my religious life. I thank God for so much historical richness and self-sacrifice that has gone into the making of my present. But I know that the superfluous layers of status, position, privilege and security must be stripped away to lay bare the power and the glory of being human and made new in the life, works, death and resurrection of Jesus Christ, Son of God and Son of Man.

Austin Smith[2]

Love is not an achievement which can be exactly defined; it is
what every man becomes when he realizes his unique essence,
something that is known only when it is done. This is not to say
that there is no general notion of love, according to the general
statement that man is obliged to love God and that this is the
fulfilment of the whole divine law and all the commandments.
For this principal commandment obliges man precisely to love
God with his whole heart. And this heart, this innermost centre
of his person and thus of whatever else belongs to the individual,
is something unique; and what is risked and given in this love is
only known afterwards, when man has found himself and truly
knows what and who he actually is. In this love, also, man is
concerned with the adventure of his own, at first concealed,
reality. He cannot estimate beforehand what is demanded of
him; for he himself is demanded, he is risked in his concrete
heart and life which are still before him as the unknown future
and which reveal only afterwards what this heart is that had to
be risked and spent in this life. In all other cases one can know
what is demanded, one can estimate, compare and ask whether
the risk is worth the gain. One can justify what has been done by
the result which turns out to make sense In the case of love this
is impossible. For it justifies itself, but it is only truly itself
when it has been perfectly achieved with all one's heart.

Fundamentally the Christian ethos is not the respect for the
objective norms with which God has endowed reality. For all
these are truly moral norms only where they express the
structure of the person. All other structures of things are below
man. He may change and transform them as much as he can, he
is their master, not their servant. The only ultimate structure of
the person which adequately expresses it is the basic power of
love, and this is without measure. Therefore man, too, is
without measure. Fundamentally all sin is only the refusal to
entrust oneself to this measurelessness, it is the lesser love
which, because it refuses to become greater, is no longer love. In
order to know what is meant by this man needs, of course, the
multiplicity of objective commandments. But whatever appears
in this multiplicity is a partial beginning of love which itself has
no norm by which it might be measured. One may speak of this
'commandment' of love if one does not forget that this 'law'

does not command something, but asks of man to be himself, that is the possibility of love by receiving God's love in which God does not give something else, but himself.

Karl Rahner[3]

CHAPTER THREE

R. C. Moberly
Ministerial Priesthood

Imagine all the truth about life, the world and the universe, our common lot, reality as a whole, discovered by humankind from the beginning up to today, being contained within one huge circle. Similar truths supporting one another gather at certain points within the circle, and contrary truths similarly gather at opposite points across it. The opposites, in fact, polarize towards the circumference and so are isolated, the more they assert their identity against one another. However, they threaten to discover new truth towards the centre the more they hold together across it, the more perhaps they immolate themselves in the fire in the crucible which is at the centre.

Now reality as we quite naturally experience it as a whole is surely one. It simply is like that, given. However, we can discern truth within the whole only by comparison and contrast with other truth. And as Carl Jung has pointed out, the circle is probably the strongest symbol that the human psyche has ever conjured up; certainly in our time it is very strong. If, then, this image expresses something fundamental, it follows that truth is always to be known in the continuing tension of thesis and antithesis, and that any hold on truth is lost, indeed all are losers, if that tension of opposites is not maintained and lived with. The opposites need each other for all or any to be in truth, and this in no way lands us in pluralism or implies that there is no place for special truth. It means, rather, that reality is continually a duality-within-unity. Now this is a very different picture from the dualism and separating off that we normally prefer.

Incidentally, the implications of such a model for ecumenicity are immense, as they also are for the party spirit which so often bedevils a mature and genuine common life and real engagement with the world's experience. At the same time the model focusses the situation of R. C. Moberly in 1897; for that was one of those many times when different 'theses' about the nature of life, of ourselves, of the church and of God were straining with each other across the centre.

For one thing, from the time of the Enlightenment in the seventeenth century, scientific and secularizing forces had been gathering strength. Most obviously there had been the impact of Newtonian physics. But in addition to this, in the eighteenth century Britain had produced a group of empiricist philosophers, the most notable of whom was perhaps the Scot David Hume, whose thrust had certainly brought down to earth much idealism and extravagant religious faith. Hume had argued that it was no longer possible to claim anything to be objective knowledge, since all that any of us can know is his or her own sense experience. With this had gone the implication that perhaps all that is, is material and secular. Furthermore, in 1859 Darwin had produced his *Origin of Species*, demonstrating that we have all in fact evolved from apes and, beyond that, literally out of the dust to which we return. Not only had Darwin's revelation, along with all that had gone before it, seemed a stunning refutation of all that Bible and church had traditionally said about human origins and that fundamental ambiguity in human life which was traditionally explained in terms of Adam's and our continuing disobedience, but all the revolutionary developments had also produced arguments in favour of a fundamentally new perspective on God and faith, related to the so-called secular laws of nature and what comes from below, particularly as a result of reason.

So in Moberly's time there was an immediate tension between the polarities of reason and revelation, science and faith, 'from below' and 'from above' – as there still is. Another tension, following directly from this, was between the traditional theology we have already been considering and what has since been called 'liberal theology'. Like most terms, this has been used in a disparaging way, often being seen as a 'weakening of true theology', when in fact what liberal theology seeks to do is to be thoroughly honest and faithful to all the truths before us, both reasoned and revealed, and not just some of them. The tension between 'liberal' theology and traditional theology was severe, and brought a good deal of pain. For example in 1853, for ideas said to be unsettling to students and particularly for refusing to believe in the traditional doctrine of everlasting damnation for those who were not Christians within the true church, F. D. Maurice, the eminent Christian theologian and socialist, had actually been deposed from his professorial chair at King's College, London. But liberal theology continued in full force and by 1880 it was attacking the very constitution of the church. For in the Bampton Lectures of that year, with a strong appeal to the increasingly powerful Free Churches who of course have traditionally emphasized simple, visible, human fellowship rather than the invisible mystical meaning of an institutional ministry, Edwin Hatch, seemingly backed by such theological giants as J. B. Lightfoot and F. W. Hort, had claimed that the ordained ministry came into being in the infant church as no more than a matter of pastoral practicality, decided by the church itself – 'in the Spirit', yes, but even so, 'from below'. Hatch had been reflecting the new discussion on the continent which had yet to be felt in England. While English theologians had generally been asking 'How is the church's ministry authorized?', German theologians had been questioning whether there was actually any justification at all in the New Testament for an institutional ministry. We shall see the reasons for this questioning in Chapter 5. For Moberly, however, such 'liberal' theology was nothing less than catastrophic, for he felt that it struck at the very heart of the true church, of which he saw himself a member, and in so doing, at the heart of the entire faith and outlook and spirit on which and for which that church stood – all 'from above'.

A third tension to be experienced in Moberly's situation was that in which his church was involved, since the Church of England was of course a state church. Moberly was living at the end of a period of confident Victorian life, of major industrial revolution, of an expanding British empire – and, presumably, of much of the kind of religious outlook and spirituality which often accompanies such things. We can see it reflected, I think, in the brass plaques from that period in those of our churches which are most 'English'. We can hear it underlying the Thatcherite call to the nation to return to 'Victorian values', and in the government's suspicion that the Church of England, the state church, is moving away from its proper position in the nation in the direction of the left.

Speaking very simply, this feeling is about such things as morality and decency and reasonableness and order and freedom for individuality and for private ownership without hindrance, and about the kind of 'belief' and 'faith' which strengthen and uphold such attitudes. This clearly domesticates the tiger of the gospel into a pussy-cat. Even apart from this, however, for church people like Moberly this state religion lacks the fundamental, constitutive element of the true church, so that it will always contain within itself a tendency towards disestablishment. Here is yet another articulation of the fundamental tension that we have already seen: between 'from above' and 'from below'. But Moberly will again want to say that while truth certainly 'comes down', 'below', its nature remains fundamentally 'from above'.

Yet a fourth tension to be experienced, but of a somewhat different kind in Moberly's situation, was from the newly born Evangelical Movement. In reaction to a secularizing spirit which seemed inevitably to lead to an undermining of revealed truth and received doctrine, to the enthronement of human reason, to atheism and to the very worst of human behaviour, and against Darwinism as a specific expression of this spirit, in this movement the Bible had been restored to the prominent position it seemed to have occupied at the Reformation. In fact there had been a good deal of the human in Martin Luther's work, reflecting another humanizing revolution of his own time. But that seems to have been lost on nineteenth-century Evangelicals. At that time the spirit of reaction, coupled with the all-pervasive influence of German idealism which in Moberly's work, as Anthony Hanson notes,[1] makes Jesus seem a heavenly bolt from the blue, together made the Bible and the church based upon it quite separate from the ordinary and the human.

While Moberly wanted to agree with the fundamental transcendence of this Evangelical position, at the same time – in
what is traditionally the Catholic spirit – he wanted to reject
what in effect was its denial of the world and of humanity. So he
gives strong emphasis to the need for incarnation, of genuine
body and structure for the church, of its concrete place in
history, of its nature of being both 'from above' and 'from
below'. So over against the Evangelical Movement, Moberly
experienced this other kind of tension. But did he in fact,
whatever his words, actually manage to maintain it? Or were he
and his church actually left in fundamentally the same separation as the Evangelicals? We shall see.

However, what finally triggered off *Ministerial Priesthood*
was an action of the Catholic Church towards the Church of
England. This is a final expression of tensions at the time, and
highlights from another direction the picture we have seen
developing. At the First Vatican Council in 1869–70 the Roman
Catholic Church, seeking to re-establish its authority, had laid
to rest hesitations about the role of the Pope and finally
established his supremacy. But of course any such move, as in
any institution, can never be a mere matter of simple organiz-
ation, authority *per se* and jurisdiction, for the way such things
are arranged inevitably creates the ethos or spirit throughout
the institution. This absolute hierarchical position of the Pope
had thus at the same time guaranteed for the whole church a
spirituality and theological outlook which was very strongly
'from above', transcendent. This spirituality and theological
outlook were particularly expressed in an understanding of the
ordained ministry on which it was fundamentally constituted
as a 'sacrificing priesthood'. Both words, as we shall see later,
again imply separation from the ordinary and the human to
centre upon what is 'from above' and, especially with the word
'sacrificing', do so in a particularly extreme way, much like the
extremeness we have just seen in the Evangelical Movement.

So it is perhaps no surprise that when in 1896 Pope Leo XIII
decisively condemned Anglican orders as null and void, the
action which finally triggered off *Ministerial Priesthood*, it did
so because they were lacking intention in ordination to ordain a
sacrificing priesthood. What Moberly wanted, from within the

church, was a church with its ordained ministry seen as priesthood and so centred upon what is 'from above', but at the same time not so extremely centred that church became sharply separated from the ordinary and the human, from the world. Moberly tried to resolve this tension by another picture of priesthood which he called 'representative', one typical of the *via media* of Anglicanism but which also maintains continuity with the ('true') Catholic church. Whether he actually resolved this tension is another matter. For as we should now be clear, from all the tensions we have examined, again and again they get pushed to breaking point, and certainly were then. At those breaking points the proper duality-within-unity breaks down into dualism, separation, absolute polarization.

So in 1897 R. C. Moberly, an outstanding theologian from the Anglo-Catholic wing of the Church of England, wrote *Ministerial Priesthood*, specifically to vindicate Anglican orders and thereby his church and its theological outlook and spirituality. It has lasted well, actually being reprinted in 1969 and having occupied an important place in theological colleges down this century, although its influence would now seem to be in decline.[2]

In his preface to the 1969 reprint, Anthony Hanson identified obvious weaknesses in method. For example, the book makes too much use of 'either-or' and the argument from silence. It is amazingly ignorant of the new biblical scholarship which had been gathering force during the nineteenth century; and in retrospect it can be seen to be substantially influenced by German idealism, with Jesus being pictured, totally without a Jewish background, as a heavenly bolt from the blue and the church as possessing a perfection from him to be transmitted as if by pipeline to subsequent generations. However, his work gave high Anglicans, Tractarians, confidence towards both the Roman Catholic Church and the state. Towards the former they could claim that they belonged to the original Catholic Church in England continuous since Augustine of Canterbury; towards the latter that it was this and not any relationship with the Crown that made them the Church of England. It also steered the *via media* typical of Anglicanism between disproportionate emphasis on eucharistic sacrifice, as characteristic of the Catholic church of the day, and the virtual denial of all such implications which is a leading characteristic of liberal Protestantism.

'The basis of true understanding of Church ministry is a true understanding of the Church,' Moberly begins. 'The Church is likened to a body; her ministers to certain specific organs or members of the body . . . So when we inquire into the rationale of church ministries, we are inquiring into the principle of the differentiation of functions within a single unity. If there are differences of ministries, if ministry, as a whole, is different from laity, these differences at once illustrate, and depend upon, the unity of that whole in which, and for which, they exist' (p. 1).

Nothing exceptional about that, the democratic mind might think. And indeed has not unity traditionally been the first of four marks of the true church? But Paul's communal model, born in a quite different time and situation, is actually a very simple one, more cell-like and much less institutionalized, more human, to do more with visible unity. Moberly is concerned for much more than that. So he is already using the word 'ministries' very differently from Paul, who sees them as different forms of locally-inspired service for the proclamation of the gospel and the upbuilding of Christian communities. By contrast, Moberly uses 'ministry' exclusively to mean the ordained threefold ministry. And because of that, and the fact that for Moberly ordained ministry symbolizes and embodies something very much more, the image of body is immediately overloaded towards breaking-point, despite the confident tone that 'these differences at once illustrate, and depend upon, the unity of that whole in which, and for which, they exist' (p. 1).

Laity will in fact be left as passive nonentities in the body, and indeed it might well be asked if they are in truth included in the church which is the primary datum. For, as I have already pointed out, Moberly is very definitely concerned for an extra dimension over and above ordinary human life. He is concerned for it because ordinary human life, as we all know, naturally lacks the unity of which he speaks and leaves us with a sense of incompleteness and lack of fundamental meaning.

Hence the distinction he now goes on to make. 'The most obvious distinction to draw is between unity acquired by degrees from below, and unity revealed as inherent from above . . . The first of these two appears, in its origin at least, to be a purely accidental unity. If this is the true account of the unity of the Church, then in the first instance there was no such thing, either in fact or ideas, as Church unity; but Christians were merely individual units, whom pressure of circumstances drove more and more to coalesce into a society, until by degrees the idea of the society became a leading idea of the Christian life. If this is historically true, then the idea of the society, exactly so far as it became among Christians religiously dominant or peremptory, is convicted of being a false idea' (pp. 2f.).

By contrast:

'The unity which the Church represents is the Unity of God. It is true therefore of the Church, in the highest conceivable sense, that her unity is not to be understood as a growth which begins from below, and gradually coalesces; her unity is not the crown of an evolution which starts from disunion; the Church is one in idea whether she is one in fact or not; her ideal unity from the first is inherent, transcendental, divine: she is one essentially, as and because God is One' (p. 6).

Now this must mean that the church cannot be only a human, visible community of the kind Paul knew; it must be invisible as well, and that brings the problems of explaining the relationship between visible and invisible, between nature and grace, and of holding them together.

Moberly ostensibly resolves his difficulty in maintaining an integrated relationship between these two dimensions by first redefining visible and invisible. His approach is clear from the title of his second chapter, 'The Relation Between Inward and Outward'. Making what would now be considered a very tendentious appeal to the New Testament, he then goes on to say: 'It cannot but occur to us in the first place that the contrast between unity of spirit, and unity of body, is not scriptural. "One Spirit; therefore not one Body" says the argument. "One Body and one Spirit" says the Scripture' (p. 31). 'It seems then to be clear that the idea of a unity which was in such sense transcendental as to dispense with the necessity of any outward expression of its ideal in the form of a practically organized and disciplined union, is an idea which never presented itself to the minds of Apostles at all. On the contrary, the more transcendental their conception of the divine unity of the Church, so much the more did it follow, as a matter of course, that the Church which expressed that unity, must be, if divinely then also humanly, if in Spirit then in body, if inwardly and invisibly then visibly and outwardly, One . . . it was the case, as emphatically then as afterwards – and as always – that the way to make spiritual ideas real, is to give them expression of reality in bodily life' (p. 34f.).

So on this view the people, what they do and what they say, the forms and structures of the church, are in a sense the very presence of God in the world and in human history. In this sense the Church can be said to be both 'from above' and 'from below', spiritual and physical, spiritual and human. But the spiritual is the essence:

'The visible body, then, of the Church, is real, and its outward process and history, as body – the history (so to speak) of its chemical analysis, or the history of its material development – are real: yet the truth of these is as untrue, in comparison with the over-mastering truth of its spiritual reality, which alone gives, even to these, their real significance: and even the very truth of these becomes a downright untruth, in so far as it ever is used, in greater measure or less, to contradict, or impair, or disguise the truth of its essential being as Spirit' (p. 41). 'If the spiritual work of the Church has instruments, organs, ordinances: if these have an existence which may be described as mechanical and material, yet their entire reality of meaning and character is spiritual' (p. 42).

What the church says and does is indeed the Kingdom of God: the church 'does not represent – but it *is* – the Kingdom of God on earth' (p. 40). Here is the traditional institutional model of the church outside which it is said that there can be no salvation, notwithstanding the ambiguity of the outward form with real 'failures and fractures' (p. 36). Here is a church too whose nature, both 'from above' and 'from below' (in the sense that Moberly means), and totally the expression of the Spirit, ought never fundamentally to be changed. Because of the absolute givenness in the nature of this church there can be no reduction of the spiritual in what Moberly calls a one-sided way to a mere individualized inner, personal communion with God typical of Protestantism. And it is undeniable that Protestants over-emphasize the inward personal communion (and salvation of 'souls') to the loss of genuine humanness and a social dimension to their theologies. Nor, for the same reason of absolute givenness, on Moberly's view can the earthly life and development of the church be understood simply in sociological terms or as the result of its own practical strategy and decisions, even if it is said to be 'in the Spirit'.

However, because what is 'beyond' and 'otherness', the holy, seem not to be present ordinarily in life but are believed to be present in the church, the institution becomes all-important and we are caught in continuing ambiguity, the more so the more idealism is at work. The ambiguity is perhaps seen more clearly when Moberly comes to the theme of the church and history. 'From above' and 'from below', spiritual and human and physical, will grow into the kingdom of God, but not 'under present conditions'.

'The Church militant does not merely *represent* the Church triumphant. The Church on earth will not be abolished and ended in order that the Kingdom of Heaven may take its place. But the Church which Christ founded on earth, which from Pentecost onwards, under all its failures and wickednesses, has yet been really the temple on earth of the Spirit – the Church disciplined, purified, perfect – shall be found to *be* the Kingdom' (p. 37).

But how will this happen? Of course this is an expression of the fundamental Christian paradox of here and not here, now and not yet, but Moberly is also at the same time in a two-world mentality of sharp separation: grace on the one hand and nature on the other; grace as an 'extra' on top of ordinary life. How can this kind of grace, said to exist exclusively in the church, ever grow into the kingdom of God? Is this true grace? Does Moberly reflect a proper duality-within-unity or decline into dualism?

I believe that the answer is made clear beyond all doubt when Moberly comes finally to focus on the ordained ministry. He took as his starting point the Church, whose fundamental mark is unity, but then he went on to an inward invisible givenness 'from above' as well. That givenness from above he now locates in the ordained ministry. There are three principles, he says, which are fundamental to an understanding of 'the indispens-ableness of consecrated "order"' (p. 66ff.).

1. The Church is a temple and a body, and that temple and body consists of all Christians: 'Most emphatically we reply that it consists of, and means, not in any way the clergy as such but the whole corporation or Church of Christ' (p. 66).

2. Ministers specifically ordained are organs of the body, 'through which the life, inherent in the total Body, expresses itself in particular functions of detail. They are organs of the whole Body, working organically for the whole Body, specific-ally representative for specific purposes and processes of the power of the life, which is the life of the whole body, not the life of some of its organs' (p. 68). This is the concept with which Moberly believes he counters the extreme 'otherness' of the Catholic church expressed in its 'sacrificing priesthood'. There is then, apparently, an equality of sorts.

But 3. As a body without eyes cannot see, without ears cannot hear, without nose cannot smell, so the rest of the body, put together, cannot carry out the special function of the ordained ministry. This is an attractive picture, with each organ performing its own functions for the whole, but it is actually seductive. For Moberly, as we have seen throughout, wants more, an 'extra' originally 'beyond' human life which is then 'given' in the institution of the church and finally becomes focussed in the ordained ministry. The separation which Moberly has presupposed all along finally comes here. It is not the church in the simple visible sense which gives the ordained ministry its character, but the ordained ministry which gives the church its character.

Crucially, the special function of the ordained ministry does not derive from the community but from beyond; if it is said to be a 'function', it is no function delegated from the community; it originates in no decision of the church itself. To explain in more detail Moberly quotes the 1868 Bampton Lectures given by his father, who was then Bishop of Salisbury, *Administration*

of the Holy Spirit: it is 'a priesthood strictly representative in its
own proper being, yet receiving personal designation and
powers, not by original derivation from the body which it
represents, or continual reference to it, but by perpetual
succession from a divine source and spring of authorizing grace'
(p. 70). Because the life which is the church must be channelled
from beyond through the ordained ministry and because it is
'beyond' and 'other', and not humanly communal, vocation and
ordination must inevitably be individualized and inward, and
indelible. Once a priest, always a priest. 'The "character" which
is conferred, and is indelible, is a status, inherently involving
capacities, duties, responsibilities of ministerial life, yet separ-
able from and in a sense external to the secret character of the
personal self, however much the inner self may be indirectly
disciplined or conditioned by it – for good or for evil' (p. 90).

The effect of the dualism inherent in this spirituality and
theological outlook is to be seen clearly when Moberly eventually comes to speak of the laity, whom he has already said are
equally organs of the one body. The chapter in which he
discusses the ordained ministry is entitled 'The Relation
between Ministry and Laity', but by the end of it the laity are left
with little identity at all. Basically, they are nonentities, second
class, passive receivers, consumers, children. Moberly quotes
Liddon, another Anglo-Catholic within the Church of England:
'If Christian laymen *would only believe with all their hearts*
that they are really priests, we should very soon escape from
some of the difficulties which vex the Church of Christ. For it
would then be seen that in the Christian church the difference
between clergy and laity is only a difference of the degree in
which certain spiritual powers are conferred; that it is not a
difference of kind' (p. 96). But the words which I have emphasized, while admittedly having a fine ring, only point out the
truth that they are no more than a turning up of volume,
whereas it is the fundamental structure which must be changed
if the laity are to be more. If the centre is 'beyond' and
'otherness', in the way, influenced by idealism, in which
Moberly conceives of these, and an 'extra' on top of ordinary life,
grace in sharp separation from nature, and if this centre is
channelled through the ordained ministry, then unless lay

people can in some way bring their own experience to engage positively with such centres, they must inevitably be left with little more than arranging flowers in church.

But this truth only highlights the larger one: that Moberly's theory as a whole is really a two-world one: of one layer upon another, human history proceeding along one, the lower one, and eternity perpetually shadowing it along the other; of nature in one and grace in the other. The picture is utterly one of separation. This is very different from the proper tension between polarities of beyond and otherness, the holy on the one hand and within and deep down in the secular on the other. This is indeed decline from duality-within-unity to dualism, as we have already seen. And since it is the ordained ministry which traditionally in Moberly's church does the theology, safeguards the tradition and has leadership, the effects of such decline are bound to be experienced in one way or another most acutely within itself and its relationships with others.

Moberly himself obviously recognizes the problem of separation, for it is that which he is attempting to resolve when finally he fixes on the image of good shepherd to express supremely what ordained ministry is: 'I do not think it is anything like a fanciful analogy to say that the perfect outward and the perfect inward, the ideal pastorate and ideal priesthood, are blended together as one indivisible reality in the words of St John, ch. 10: "I am the good shepherd: the good shepherd layeth down his life for the sheep"' (p. 294). It is, of course, a paternalistic image, relating to the 'Father' and to the 'beyond'. It holds the tension, he says, because the essence of being the good shepherd 'in the sphere of sin' is sacrifice and love. 'Love is not self-contained, but self-expending, and perfected in self-expenditure. The devotion of love in the sphere of Heaven is perfection of joy. But devotion of love to another in conditions of earth – even whilst it touches the highest possibilities of joy – means always more or less of pain. Devotion of self, in a world of sin and suffering, to the spiritual welfare of those who are enmeshed in suffering and sin, is forthwith, in eternal aspect, sacrifice; and, in inner essence, love. There is no essential contrast between sacrifice and love. Love, under certain disabling conditions, becomes sacrifice; and sacrifice is not sacrifice, except it be love' (p. 247f.)

This moving expression of an insight which has given marvellous inspiration to countless Christians and particularly those in the ordained ministry down the years is surely true. But love and sacrifice need proper structure, else, as in much of the modern context, they become exhausted or die for rarely being expressed. Moberly's context and structure spring from what he in fact sees as 'disabling conditions' and from his vision of 'the Church as a small kernel or focus of brightness in the midst of the world . . . I say that the thought of the church as a spot of light in the midst of surrounding darkness illustrates the conception of her priestliness' (p. 256). While most of us will recognize truth in this kind of picture, it can scarcely express in modern times that which is unique and distinctive in Christian life. In modern times that truth must be brought back into tension with other more all-embracing truth. On its own, it leaves us in a position in which we can never engage at all with the facts and problems of Chapter 2 and much else today besides, most notably ecumenicity.

Second Interlude

On a dangerous seacoast where shipwrecks often occur there was once a crude little life-saving station. The building was just a hut, and there was only one boat, but the few devoted members kept a constant watch over the sea, and with no thought of themselves went out day and night tirelessly searching for the lost. Many lives were saved by this wonderful little station, so that it became famous. Some of those who were saved, and various others in the surrounding area, wanted to become associated with the station and give of their time and money and effort for the support of its work. New boats were bought and new crews trained. The little life-saving station grew.

Some of the members of the life-saving station were unhappy that the building was so crude and poorly equipped. They felt that a more comfortable place should be provided as the first refuge of those saved from the sea. So they replaced the emergency cots with beds and put better furniture in the enlarged building. Now the life-saving station became a popular gathering place for its members, and they decorated it beautifully and furnished it exquisitely, because they used it as a sort of club. Fewer members were now interested in going to sea on life-saving missions, so they hired lifeboat crews to do this work. The life-saving motif still prevailed in this club's decoration, and there was a liturgical lifeboat in the room where the club initiations were held. About this time a large ship was wrecked off the coast, and the hired crews brought in boatloads of cold, wet, and half-drowned people. They were dirty and sick, and some of them had black skin and some had yellow skin. The beautiful new club was in chaos. So the property committee immediately had a shower house built outside the club where victims of shipwreck could be cleaned up before coming inside.

At the next meeting, there was a split in the club membership. Most of the members wanted to stop the club's life-saving activities as being unpleasant and a hindrance to the normal social life of the club. Some members insisted upon life-saving as their primary purpose and pointed out that they were still called a life-saving station. But they were finally voted down and told that if they wanted to save the lives of all the various kinds of people who were shipwrecked in those waters, they could begin their own life-saving station down the coast. They did.

As the years went by, the new station experienced the same changes that had occurred in the old. It evolved into a club, and yet another life-saving station was founded. History continued to repeat itself, and if you visit that sea coast today, you will find a number of exclusive clubs along that shore. Shipwrecks are frequent in those waters, but most of the people drown!

Richard Wheatcroft/Theodore Wedel[1]

His study in the Albertinum, on the ground floor, looks out on to a park filled with trees, grassy lawns and flowers. In the room itself, if you are fortunate enough to visit it, or in pictures taken at interviews given in it, one can see how plants also invade the house, bringing a life of their own to a place where books seem so predominant. Schillebeeckx would not be happy without them; he is not a theologian oblivious of his surroundings or of all the good things the world has to offer: it is not part of creation faith to ignore the good things that God has made. And that combination of deep thought, faith, and love of the living beauty of nature seems an appropriate combination for a great theologian. So let that be the point at which we leave him.

Except for one last parable. We saw at the start how fond Schillebeeckx is of striking illustrations and modern parables. He is the author of this particular one, but it has never appeared in print because for once it is one which he acted out rather than wrote.

He once came to stay as a guest in my home. On the morning of his departure he mysteriously went out and came back again, to go out a second time an hour or so later. When he returned, he was clutching a large bunch of quite beautiful flowers which he handed over to us as a token of thanks. His concern that thought should be extended to careful, well-considered praxis proved to have covered even this kind gesture. As we discovered later, he had gone to the florist's twice. The first time the flowers in the shop were not as fresh as he would have liked, so having ascertained that there was to be a further delivery later in the morning, he went back to ensure that the ones he bought were fresh. They lasted longer than any other bunch we have ever been given.

John Bowden[2]

CHAPTER FOUR

Yves Congar
Lay People in the Church

'I look upon the world as my parish.' The words are John Wesley's, but they provide the dedication of a little book published in Britain in 1961, originating in an earlier series of articles in France by the Catholic Dominican Yves Congar.[1] A photograph of the earth's surface from an Atlas missile dominates the cover. So this is a very different world from that of Moberly. Two wars have devastated Europe, in particular, since then, and at the same time have devastated ideals. Man now knows the hideous strength of evil and destruction. However, the Second World War over, nations have been struggling to rebuild. The old colonizing nations have been losing empires and struggling for new identity. War may be past, but the Cold War is on between the ideologies of capitalism and communism, with new, devastating technological dimensions. Advances in communication have brought awareness of the many other inhabitants of a global village. The poor and hungry have come within the vision of Western eyes, and among them Marxism will find open ears. Britain will be told 'You've never had it so good', as it reaps the material benefits of technology along with others. But as well as this very changed world, in Western cultures at least there is again great movement, a great ferment of ideas, from the gathering scientific and humanizing revolution. It is as if a whole welter of factors have converged to challenge men and women to step forward into a new kind of humanity more at the centre of life and more responsible for it themselves.

And for the church, if all this were not challenge enough, there are challenges too from the now-unavoidable biblical scholarship of the preceding half-century which, in short, brings down to earth the earlier idealism to be seen in Moberly; and challenges from the now-unavoidable presence of other churches and other faiths, religious and political, and none. The Roman Catholic Church in particular will experience challenges just like that from evolutionary Darwinism in the time of Moberly, now from the work of its own theologian and anthropologist Teilhard de Chardin. As with similar work before, his will be banned for being too evolutionary, too optimistic, too liberal, effectively 'from below'; but the way in which Christianity is pointed towards both material and cosmic dimensions will be undeniable for all that.

'Christians,' Congar prefaces his book, 'have simultaneously become newly-conscious of their minority position in the world and of the absolutely universal character of God's "plan". At a time when this minority position and the daily pressure of Communism are in a measure driving them to take their faith really seriously, and when the liturgical movement and the biblical renewal are giving them back a sense of the Lord's total absolute sovereignty, at this moment they are also strongly experiencing the call of a world that has to be built up . . . For thoughtful people the problems of salvation and of the salvation of "the others" have thus become a constant subject of inquiry . . . The divided world in which we live requires that we should be very careful to maintain the integrity of our attitudes, but it ought also to be a world of exchange of ideas and co-operation. So there ought to be sections of this chapter headed Oecumenism, Conditions for "pluralism" and human co-operation in a spiritually divided world, Tolerance, Possibility of a "Christian politics", and so forth' (pp. ixf.).

The world, then, hand in hand with shifts in Christian understanding, is driving the church out of itself, and one revolutionary expression of it in France is the birth of the worker-priest movement. But how far in fact is it right for anyone to go in this direction, if Christian life is understood as fundamentally 'from above'? Congar is critically concerned to

avoid what he calls the superficial, 'if not disastrous', 'reconciliation' of science and religion characteristic of liberal
theologians from the end of the nineteenth century. Doubtless
he will have had in mind the crisis experienced by Karl Barth in
his Germany of the 1920s and 1930s, causing him to turn his
back utterly on the natural theology he had been schooled in,
for a fundamental restatement of a theology of transcendence.
In the context of the developing National Socialist state and
Hitler's emerging evils, Barth had found his liberal natural
theology quite inadequate. Nonetheless, to be 'cut off from the
outside world and in ignorance of the interests and upheavals
of human society is a positively fantastic idea' (p. 7). 'It may be
that the religion of the classical epoch was characterized by a
certain individualism: Peter Nicole (d. 1695), for example,
declared that "A man is created to live alone with God for
ever". A possible comment on this nowadays is one that would
have astonished and even scandalized Nicole: Save my soul
alone? No, it shall be all or one! Whilst not going so far as that,
this feeling for human solidarity certainly haunts many
Christian consciences today' (p. 6). It begins to strain the
tension between 'from above' and 'from below' to breaking
point again, for there can be no way in which the former as
traditionally seen by Moberly and the latter, identified with
the world at large, can be held together.

However, it was to be this new spirit which would inspire the
calling of the Second Vatican Council in 1962, in which Congar
was to be one particularly strong influence. To understand the
context and the character of this council is thus to understand
more of Congar's work.

When John XXIII, just two years after his accession, an-
nounced the calling of Vatican II, it was, Christopher Butler
remarks, 'more than a little sensational, the more so since he
seemed to link this project with the prospect of Christian, not
merely Catholic unity'.[2] What was its purpose, though? 'Nothing in particular, it would appear; or perhaps it would be truer
to say: everything . . . (the) immediate aim was to let some fresh
air into the Church and to promote within her an *ag-
giornamento*,' a bringing-up-to-date. However, reflecting the
tension between 'from above' and 'from below' yet again: 'There

were in fact two sides to Catholicism in 1960. While the Curia gave little evidence of realizing the need for far-reaching changes, the church as a whole, and particularly in Western Europe north of the Alps, had for some time been experiencing a second spring . . . so that when the Council met in 1962 there were . . . not only the canon lawyers and strict Thomists who enjoyed the favour of the Curia but a host of others of a very different type, including men like de Lubac, Karl Rahner and Congar, who had all suffered for their convictions but who became in fact in large measure the artificers of the theology of Vatican II' (pp. 13–15).

Of course the two sides still exist today; indeed many would say that the strong influence of the present Pope has shifted the balance back the other way, now re-emphasizing beyond and otherness to the detriment of proper concern for the ordinary and the human. Then, however, while reaffirming the tradition, the theology of the Council reached out a long way beyond it. A church which had traditionally regarded itself as the true church and others as apostate, with ministries that were null and void, now affirmed the credibility of the churches of the Reformation. The truth was now said to subsist in the Catholic church, implying that it existed beyond its boundaries. Indeed, the truth was reflected in other world faiths, and even in people of no conscious faith, who could nevertheless be said to be 'seeking God in shadows and images', and in the sincerity of their lives and actions.[3] A church which had traditionally regarded the truth as virtually exclusively located in its priesthood or ordained ministry now aimed at releasing the gifts and energies of lay people for a ministry which in some sense was thought of as belonging to all.

Traditionally, membership of this church had been seen in terms of belonging to the institution called the Body of Christ, belonging within the ark of salvation. But now the rediscovery of a new image of belonging to the church was held in tension with that one, the image of the people of God. This now implied that membership was to be more 'democratized', with equality of responsibility between priesthood and laity. Membership of the church was to be a matter of being more human, more visible, more active, particularly more active in the world at large, and, and, as with Israel on pilgrimage through the wilderness, one never arrived but had constantly to be on the move.

In France in 1951 Congar had already written a major work, in response to increasing demand for a thoroughgoing theology of laity, and it surely provided the substance of this part of the Council's work. Significantly it was reissued in slightly revised form in 1964 at the end of the Council. This is the book that we shall be examining in this chapter.[4]

Congar begins with an anecdote, published fifty years previously, in Moberly's time, in a Catholic Truth Society pamphlet. 'An inquirer asked a priest what was the position of the layman in the Catholic church. "The layman has two positions," answered the priest. "He kneels before the altar; that is one. And he sits below the pulpit; that is the other." The author of the pamphlet had added that there is a third that the priest had forgotten: the layman also puts his hand in his purse.'

Congar goes on: 'In a sense that is still so, and always will be so ... Lay people will always be a subordinate order in the Church; but they are on the way to the recovery of a fuller consciousness of being organically active members thereof, by right and in fact ... We can see signs of this everywhere' (p. xi).

Laity, then, are to be fully recognized; not in status so much as in the dignity of their responsibility to be 'active'. Already from this beginning we should see clearly the polarities which will almost certainly leave Congar in the position Moberly was in, and so unable to fulfil his task. The frustration will be experienced around the word 'active'. For on Congar's presuppositions about church and ordained ministry the only activity which can be left to laity is again being the recipients of much louder statements about themselves and their role. Congar is well aware of the separation responsible for this. 'Many people do not realize sufficiently that a big space is left empty between, on the one hand, a rigid canonical attitude in sacred things, wherein all the emphasis is on the receptive attitude of the faithful and their subordination to the clergy, and, on the other hand, the field of social and international secular activity' (p. xv). Everywhere there is a request for a proper

theology of the laity. 'So far-reaching a request is not met
simply by putting out a number of special theses on particular
points. The requirement is very closely bound up with so many
problems . . . such matters as the relations of the Church and
the world, an up-to- date pastoral theology, formation of the
clergy and the meaning of their priesthood, the nature of the
laity's obligation, the Christian meaning of history and of
earthly realities . . . But its central problem goes beyond the
sum of these big questions . . . and that is a "total ecclesiology".'
Indeed everything, every issue raised here goes back to what we
understand the church to be.

But what actually is a lay person? For a definition Congar goes
first to the Bible. In the Old Testament, he notices, our
traditional distinction between clerical and lay is never to be
found. Lay actually relates to the *laos*, who are the people of
Israel having a special relationship to God as a whole. The
function of priests is within the whole. In the New Testament,
priestly themes are taken over from the Old, but again no
distinction is made between clerical and lay, the term again
being applied to the people as a whole. This is a startling fact,
Congar acknowledges, which needs accounting for. It is so
prominent that since the Reformation Protestant theologians
have been arguing that in fact in the beginning the church had
no priestly structure, being undifferentiated in membership,
with a purely charismatic order, a priesthood simply for all
believers. On this view Christ had fulfilled the old ways with
God by doing away with them, contrary to the idea of his having
filled them with what they had previously lacked and so having
carried them over. He had superseded the shadows of religious
practices with life itself in all its fullness. It might seem that
this interpretation of the New Testament is reinforced by later
evidence about Christian ritual. That ritual was of course
needed, as in almost every area of human life, to express and
realize this new life, but what was remarkable about the early
Christians up to the second century was the modesty of their
ritual. By contrast with contemporary religions, they were
commonly called atheists, because they actually had no
sacrifices, and were accused before emperors because of this.
Here is certainly a point with major implications for the way in

which the church has subsequently developed and the recent problems it has encountered as a result.

Congar accounts for the startling evidence from the Bible in much the same way as Moberly and all others who are concerned for a pipeline concept of 'apostolic succession'. By AD 96, he argues, in a letter from Clement to the church in Corinth, there is first evidence of the use of the words 'layman' and 'priest' in distinction from each other, and from the beginning of the third century this distinction abounds in the church in both East and West, though the inclusive use of *laos*, people, is still known. Of course the evidence from Clement is thin enough as it is to serve as support for the traditional view to which Congar is wedded. The evidence he presents subsequently could itself argue for the opposite view. If the use of *laos* for the people as a whole was still widespread, just how should 'distinction' be interpreted? Modern biblical scholarship would certainly point in this direction, and show that such presentation is tendentious, though of course important for a fundamentalist, pipeline concept of apostolicity 'perpetually' confirming the church in its *status quo* 'from above'.

Congar goes on to point out how subsequently the distinction extends to provide for three states for Christians, and this is the church's permanent pattern: the lay, the clerical and the monastic, within the whole people of God. For Congar historical pressures, like the apparent failure of the Second Coming and the influence of imperial society on the church in its development of a hierarchical structure, are ultimately only 'incidental' (in the strictest sense); they are the historical context in which the very essence of Christian life which was from the beginning came to be forced out into the open and at last shown for what it fundamentally is. Because Congar is concerned to demonstrate such an 'essence' in Christian life, he also revives an old argument about the relationship between the authority of scripture and that of church tradition and allows the latter to interpret the former.

For Congar, Christian life is, of course, 'from above'. Here we can have no abiding city. Christ himself came 'from above'. The phenomenon of monasticism in the church from the fourth century onwards, the flight from the city into the desert,

confirms these truths in a permanent pattern. And the fundamental questions which are begged by such assumptions are
not asked or even recognized. What is the meaning of the
experience of having no abiding city here? Does the experience
in fact require us to enter an institution from which to look
'above' the world? How is religious language being used when
the New Testament says that Christ came 'from above'? After
all, whatever else, Christ is Jesus, a man. What idealism is in
fact at work here? For all his genuine concern for laity and for
the world, Congar is still trapped in the traditional position.
True, he is beginning to recognize problems, but he cannot
actually find a way of resolving them.

So when he comes next to amplifying the permanent pattern
of the three states of Christians, who are at the same time all
part of the one people of God, his work is as full of ambiguity as
Moberly's. 'The lay condition is *not so much a matter of a
definition* as of something immediately given as a basis, the
condition of Christians who are working out their salvation in
the everyday life of the world' (pp. 6f.) And priests, bishops and
Pope are indeed laymen first of all. By saying this, Congar
reaffirms the idea of the whole people of God, the *laos*. 'The
clerical condition *is defined* by the service of the altar and the
religious service of the Christian people. Clericature itself is
then an office, a function, not a state of life.' This is a modest
way of speaking, intended to reinforce the first idea. As an 'office
or function', and not a state or status, priesthood is intended to
be held within the whole. The idea of service is the concept by
which Congar hopes to do this. The monastic condition '*is not
defined by an office or function, but as a state or way of life*: in
order that he shall not live for the world and in the world's way
but rather so much as possible for God and in God's way' (pp.
6f.). The italics here are mine, because this highly revealing
summary points us to the heart of Congar's theology, demonstrating the tensions he is having to work with and showing
why ultimately he cannot resolve them in any satisfactory way.
First, though his aim is to create a thoroughgoing theology for
the laity, so that they can be active in the world, Congar cannot
actually provide any definition of them worthy of the name. We
shall see why in a moment.

By contrast, however, priesthood *can* be defined, by the altar and the religious service of the Christian people. Some modern lay Christians and indeed some priests might by contrast define themselves by their house churches and basic communities and by service of an altar set within the world. But already we can begin to see why Congar finds laity hard to define: because they are implicitly defined in terms of the definition he *can* make, that of priesthood, what he emphasizes is service. But then, both laity and priesthood are themselves together implicitly defined in terms of a third state, the monastic condition, which is indeed said to be a state and not a function. That, according to Congar, is the state in which God is best known and served, in separation from the world. Incidentally, it is worth noting that although nuns occasionally get a mention, it is monks who dominate the monastic condition. This is surely a reflection of a kind of 'beyond' and 'otherness' naturally expressed in maleness rather than femaleness. The crucial point, however, is that if the centre of the church, the whole people of God, is to be located in what the monastic condition stands for, the laity cannot possibly be defined. How can that kind of holiness live with the ordinary and the human?

Ironically, Congar actually recognizes the historical assimilation of the clerical to the monastic, and the inevitable effect this has had upon both the image of the church and the position of the laity. He first notes the 'monastic notion' in which 'the distinction is made in terms of states of life, of the manner or means of sanctification. Clerics and monks are men given over to the holy, so far as may be they live in the divine world. The laity lives among earthly things.' However, with this went two unacceptable implications: 'the lay position is presented as a concession (to human weakness) and its general tendency is to deny that the laity, concerned in temporal affairs, have any active part in the sphere of sacred things'. Then there is the 'canonical notion' that the clergy have not only to live by faith but also to impart it, and the laity become defined in terms of lacking this competence.

But notwithstanding his recognition of these things, Congar cannot actually break out of the presuppositions in which he is trapped. So when he finally tries to say what a lay person is, he can only 'outline' it in terms of two 'approximations', full of ambiguity and still dominated by a concessionary tone. Certainly Congar rejects the view that 'clerics and monks are by their state and directly, ordered to heavenly things; lay people are, by their state and directly (though not exclusively), ordered to earthly things. But it is true to say that: 1. Lay people do not live exclusively for heavenly things; that is, so far as present circumstances allow, the condition of monks. 2. Lay people are Christians to the fullest extent as touching life in Christ, but they have no competence, or only a limited competence, touching the properly ecclesial means to life in Christ; these means belong to the competence of clerics ... The laity's relation to the one last end is perhaps less immediate, certainly less exclusive, than that of clergy and monks; but it partakes of theirs in a secondary sense ...' (pp. 18ff.)

More promisingly for a genuinely lay spirituality, he says that for the lay person the substance of things themselves is 'real and interesting', something that clerics and monks can lose sight of. The cleric runs the risk of ignoring the process of history and world and of forgetting, even more, that things do exist. 'It is against the confiscation of the internal truth of second causes by the First Cause that modern laicism rebelled; fundamentally it was a movement to recapture rights in second causes, that is, in earthly things' (pp. 21f.). But no sooner has he expressed this crucial insight than he falls back into his traditional position by saying that for clerics and monks things are real and interesting only within their relationship to God. Congar's assumptions about 'God' here are, of course, crucial, but he does not examine them.

So for Congar ordinary things cannot yet be seen as truly sacramental; that is, as reflecting, speaking of and symbolizing the living presence of God. For him, they are still largely eschatological; that is, only pointing to what is ultimately 'beyond', 'above', and at worst a mere backcloth for salvation, and so basically there to be 'denied'. For Congar, therefore, 'beyond' and 'otherness' are the essentials. And consequently the laity cannot be other than left as they were before, with no real place in the church, or indeed in the world, and virtually no theology to speak of.

The essential spirit of 'beyond' and 'otherness' is revealed again and again in Congar's subsequent account, first of all in his description of the church. Like Moberly, he describes one reality with two aspects, visible and invisible, and for the self-same reasons. Salvation 'from above' was given by God to the 'fallen' world in the incarnation. Christ gave salvation, God's very presence, to the church he is seen as having founded. Indeed from the beginning the forms and structures in which this salvation 'from above' came to be expressed in what was 'from below' have been 'ontological', the way things actually are, as a matter of essential being. This church and this salvation have been transmitted down succeeding generations in turn, in unbroken continuity to the present time. And the outward and visible forms express and contain the inward and the invisible.

Incidentally, this theological outlook demonstrates how the Catholic church has traditionally insisted, as a matter of life and death, that sacraments work *ex opere operato*, that is to say, just by doing them. Protestants have traditionally suspected this view of grace as being mechanical and magical, impersonal and requiring no true repentance. At best, there is the great truth here of the immediacy of God's presence, requiring no more from a sinner than that he or she simply turn and repent. At best, then, it is pure gospel. But even this, we are bound to say, comes within the framework of presuppositions which have given rise to this particular church. And as with Moberly, these are still fundamentally 'from above' and exclusive to the institution, whatever the obvious concern for laity and the world at large. What kind of 'gospel', then, can this be?

Interestingly, Congar criticizes Karl Barth for lacking a fundamental structure of the church in his theology and reducing God's presence in the world to merely inward and invisible 'acts' and 'events' occurring in individual hearts (pp. 42f.). In that case the church is reduced to a mere fellowship of believers. And surely it is undeniable that Protestant churches have traditionally lacked earthedness and fleshliness and body and structure. At the Reformation, Congar concedes, 'a certain one-sidedness' had developed which caused Protestants to reduce church in this way to inward Christianity, thus dissolving a proper ecclesiology. But this also caused Catholics for their part to reduce the church to a hierarchical machinery of grace which, *in extremis*, could carry on without laity at all. On the one hand there were people without priesthood; on the other, there was priesthood without people. In an important observation Congar is here obviously striving to close the gap between outward structure and inward inspiration, between the institution and the human, and in this, incidentally, he forwards the cause of ecumenicity. But at the same time he also begs the very question he set himself to answer from the beginning of his work, that of the place of lay people in the world. For the Reformation, as he himself acknowledges, was originally about precisely this reassertion of the dignity of the human, about bringing holiness out of the cloister and into the world. But what kind of humanness was being implied, and to what extent was holiness entering the world? The truth is that both Catholic and Reformed traditions, as we saw in the previous chapter, have since then largely maintained a sharp separation from full humanness and the world at large, because they have both understood themselves fundamentally as being 'from above', and the greater the unseen influence of idealism, as we saw with Moberly, the sharper the separation. Significantly, by the way, those whose task it has been to safeguard this faith, in priesthood or ordained ministry, have traditionally been trained on idealist, or metaphysical, presuppositions. In neither tradition, then, has the full implication been recognized and received of the place of the laity in a church whose fundamental characteristic is the experience of existence in ordinary life. Congar is simply one instance of this situation.

The next step in Congar's theology, when he moves on from the church to look directly at the world, reveals exactly the same position. Like Moberly, he says that there are three realities: kingdom, church and world. But because he is far more concerned for the world, he sees the kingdom in much wider terms than Moberly, for whom it is the end-point and consummation of the *church's* history, though at the same time it is in some sense the world. Here, true to Congar's concern, the kingdom is said to be the end-point and consummation of the whole creation. So in the incarnation God is not merely said to have sent down salvation 'from above' and to have founded the church as his presence in the world but, by taking human flesh, is said now to have given all humanity new dignity and power within a world made God's own. Christ is now Lord of all creation, as the New Testament itself indicates. The world may be still sinful, but there is a sense in which the whole of creation has now been fundamentally redeemed.

This shift of position is reflected in the difference in the significance which Congar and Moberly attach to the form and structures of the church. For Moberly they must finally be gathered up as 'given', and completed; Congar can sit somewhat more lightly to them. However, if creation has now been redeemed as a whole, and yet is sinful, what are the implications? The Bible, Congar continues, clearly sees two stages in human history. There is the first achievement by which nature throughout the cosmos has been reconciled with grace. With it has begun the renewing of the kingdom. With it fellowship with God is actually present in the world. With it Spirit is within matter; grace and nature are no longer separate realities, but nature is now 'graced'. With it – and here we have an echo of the contemporary visions of the evolutionary Teilhard de Chardin and the revolutionary dialectic of Marxism – human nature, human history and the very material of the cosmos are all transfigured to point towards the ultimate consummation of Christofinalization (pp. 71, 115). In this light, then, the ordinary things of life ought now to be seen as genuinely sacramental and not merely eschatological, certainly 'real and interesting'. The second achievement will be final, total: consummation itself, as pointed to in the great biblical images of bride, body, city and temple.

But separating these two achievements there is a 'space between' during which the church, the people of God, knows the kingdom only by faith and in hope. In this time God awaits man's genuine co-operation. The consummation of the redemption already won is inevitable, but human co-operation has a bearing on the result (pp. 103f., where delightful images like that of the master and the student point to a genuinely graced nature. But the truth about Congar's theology proves to be quite different.) In this time, Christ is known more as priest than as king, more as victim and sacrifice. Triumph is by a cross, for all that Christ also reigns 'in heaven'. However, though most of us would recognize in such claims the here-and-yet-not-here character of being a Christian in ordinary life, is this genuinely what Congar is describing? Is he describing a proper duality-within-unity, or is it rather that whatever they may say, his words are concealing a dualism? Has he genuinely moved out of the separated two-world mentality of grace and nature? Are the things of ordinary life here and now sacramental and not merely eschatological? Is the cosmos actually redeemed, while being sinful?

The problem for Congar is still the one we saw with Moberly. The fundamental centre is 'beyond' and 'otherness' as located exclusively in the 'given' institution of the church, and finally of course in the priesthood or ordained ministry. Separation is inevitably heightened under the unseen influence of idealism, the metaphysical. And how can the kind of holiness necessitated by such a framework ever get back into ordinary life, whatever words are used? Indeed the very words 'get back' themselves reveal the presuppositions and the problem, suggesting that God is to be taken to the world, whereas Congar has first said that the world has been redeemed, that nature now is 'graced'. The dualism in which Congar is in fact still trapped becomes clear when he returns to the position of the church in the ostensibly redeemed creation. There is, he says, 'on the one side a universe over which Christ is king but does not reign, and on the other a *church* (italics mine) over which Christ is king and over which he does reign' (pp. 79). Admittedly there are delicate tensions to be held in being between kingdom, church and world, but Congar's fundamental emphasis on church has in fact destroyed them. Jesus himself, he then says in a revealing way, separated 'apostolic' from temporal dominion and refrained from giving the church authority in temporal affairs. We therefore need to beware of simply carrying over Christian order to things temporal, as do Jehovah's Witnesses and Bible students, Tolstoyism and its expression in the movement for non-violence (which was then prominent) (pp. 107f.).

Now certainly there is a continuing problem of how to interpret Christian tradition and 'apply' it to modern situations; for instance, how is the injunction to turn the other cheek to be 'applied' to East-West relations today? But in no way can Jesus' life and vision of the kingdom be said to have dualistically separated 'apostolic' from temporal dominion. In the Gospels there is experience of separation in human terms with the deepest fundamental meaning, but in no way does this imply separation into two worlds. That would have been unthinkable to the Jewish and Christian mind. Congar is therefore interpreting the New Testament on his own presuppositions which we have already recognized, and which are revealed again here in phrases like 'separated "apostolic" from temporal', 'carrying Christian order to things temporal'. These, of course, are also the presuppositions which have recently given rise to the claim that church and politics do not belong together. So when finally Congar turns back to the integration of church and world necessitated by his understanding of the incarnation and then of one world of graced nature, we find an ambiguity to which it is impossible to attach any adequate meaning. There is no total discontinuity between church and world, nor too much continuity, but 'a certain continuity . . . which the dualistic-eschatological position misses', arising out of 'God's unitary plan' (p. 87).

The truth is that, whatever Congar's words and whatever his purpose, he cannot escape the dualism his presuppositions must entail. Consequently lay people can only be the objects of ministry yet again, and cannot genuinely be 'active'. They may be like, as Congar describes them in a moving image, the maquis of the world (pp. 107f.), but it is significant that here he actually shifts the meaning from withdrawal and subversion to 'mixing' with the world. The evidence of his theology is that this mix would prove very weak, so weak that people will eventually cease to listen; the church is left with a sense that something is still fundamentally wrong, and lay people in particular are perhaps made to bear a sense of not really being at home in either of two separated worlds. Perhaps lay people too are still not much more than what they ultimately were for

Moberly; nonentities, second class, passive recipients, consumers, even children, who have their 'fathers' and cannot
have God for their Father unless they are mothered by the
church.

Third Interlude

Above and below are bound to one another. The word of him who wishes to speak with men without speaking with God is not fulfilled; but the word of him who wishes to speak with God without speaking with men goes astray.

There is a tale that a man inspired by God once went out from the creaturely realms into the vast waste. There he wandered till he came to the gates of the mystery. He knocked. From within came the cry: 'What do you want here?' He said: 'I have proclaimed your praise in the ears of mortals, but they were deaf to me. So I came to you that you yourself may hear me and reply.' 'Turn back,' came from within. 'Here is no ear for you, I have sunk my hearing into the deafness of mortals.'

True address from God directs man into the place of lived speech, where the voices of the creatures grope past one another, and in their very missing of one another succeed in reaching the eternal partner.

Martin Buber[1]

It is this real love for God that must be kept in view, as we now proceed to ask ourselves about the relationship between love for God and love for neighbour. It is this true, genuine love of God that we shall be speaking of, and not some individual, particular moral exploit.

The relationship of the love of God to a love of neighbour is not merely in virtue of the fact that a love of neighbour is commanded by it and functions somehow as a practical test case for it. The relationship is much more intimate than that. Love of God and love of neighbour stand in a relationship of mutual conditioning. Love of neighbour is not only a love that is demanded by the love of God, an achievement flowing from it; it is also in a certain sense its antecedent condition.

This relationship of mutual conditioning, of mutual inclusion, must not of course be understood in the sense of a secular humanism, as if love for God were only an old-fashioned, mythological expression for love of neighbour – so that, when all is said and done, one could simply skip over it today if one could still maintain an inexorable, unselfish love for human beings without it. No, God is more than a human being – infinitely more. He is the loving God to whom the human being reaches out in adoration across all human reality. And yet a mutual relationship does obtain between love of God and love of neighbour, in their real mutual conditioning. There is no love for God that is not, in itself, already a love for neighbour; and love for God only comes to its own identity through its fulfilment in a love for neighbour. Only one who loves his or her neighbour can know who God actually is. And only one who ultimately loves God (whether he or she is reflectively aware of this or not is another matter) can manage unconditionally to abandon himself or herself to another person, and not make that person the means of his or her own self-assertion.

Karl Rahner[2]

CHAPTER FIVE

Edward Schillebeeckx
The Church with a Human Face

Theology, properly understood, is just as much a science and just as objective and subject to principles of logic as the so-called natural sciences, though its framework, being the totality of life, its assumption of 'faith' and its method, in no way that of a laboratory situation, are of course all different in character. However, again just like the natural sciences, theology cannot be purely objective. It can never be about God or ultimate reality in himself, herself or itself, but only about those as they are thought about, experienced and reflected on by people. However objective we may be, theology in the nature of the case cannot but be about God-for-us. To acknowledge this is by no means to imply that God is necessarily a figment of our own imagination or a mere projection of ourselves, though this may happen to be the case. It does, however, imply that we should expect to find personalities, cultures, concerns, points in history reflected in theology; indeed, we should expect to find them actually giving shape to ultimate reality at those points where transcendent and immanent, beyond and within, converge upon each other and coincide in a proper tension.

Recovery of this understanding has been a major contribution of much modern theology, fundamentally altering the way Bible and church tradition have normally been looked upon. So with our two previous theologians, continuing a tradition in the West lasting a millennium, for a while it was thought that was of primary importance. One tended to think one's way to God and then 'believed'. Theology was largely deductive, an academic discipline. Because rationality by nature leads 'out there', God was seen as 'above', 'beyond', and his institutions had the same perspective. The faith was taught and learned, and then had to be applied back to ordinary life. 'Believing' was the church's central pastoral aim. 'Tradition', mediating experience of God 'out there', was something essentially to be preserved. All this was 'God-for-us' in their times. But in the modern world experiencing has come largely to displace pure thinking. And so God must now be experienced before he can be believed in. Theology is to be a reflective discipline based on experience, inductive. 'Tradition' is, rather, to be something to be held in tension with experience so that tradition and experience may mutually highlight one another and actually develop the tradition. Because experiencing by nature goes 'down deep', God is to be found more 'within' life, and again the same is true of his institutions. The faith which before had to be taught and learned and then 'applied' to ordinary life is now more to be intuited from within it. And because that is the case, rightly understood, it has the capacity for change.

We saw a good deal of the historical context and concerns of the first two theologians we considered, and from those, in conjunction with their work, we could perhaps have intuited much of their personalities. With our third theologian, however, we have not only the advantage of familiarity with a historical context which is more or less ours as well, but also insight into his personality and experience through a particularly perceptive biography by John Bowden.[1] Sensitively listened to, they point to the very different 'God-for-us' in modern times running through his work.

Edward Schillebeeckx was born in 1914 into a Belgian Catholic family and since the age of nineteen has been a Dominican, like Yves Congar; for thirty years he has been professor of theology at the University of Nijmegen, in the Netherlands. The continuing importance to him of his ordination within the Catholic church is reflected in the dating of a foreword to the first relatively small but revolutionary book he wrote on *Ministry* by 'The anniversary of my ordination to the priesthood'. The precise significance of that ordination will prove a crucial matter.

By 1968, John Bowden says in his portrait of the man, 'Schillebeeckx . . . had made a considerable reputation in Roman Catholic circles as a gifted creative theologian who had proved an invaluable adviser to the Dutch bishops and had done important interpretative and critical work on an unofficial basis during the Second Vatican Council. Above all, he was known for his fresh and imaginative reinterpretation of the sacraments, much influenced by existentialism . . . It had made Schillebeeckx an international theologian's theologian . . . (and) because of his many appearances, giving lectures or appearing on television, Schillebeeckx, an attractive and likeable person, had shown that he had something to say to men and women in the modern world' (p. 1). However, 'by 1979 much of this had changed. Thanks to the disclosure of the investigation going on into the orthodoxy of some of the content of his substantial book *Jesus* which had appeared in the meanwhile, in circumstances the apparent injustice of which shocked the public world-wide, Schillebeeckx had become a symbol, even to those who were not church members, of that right of Catholic theologians to study their subject freely in an academic setting . . . to the countless petitions started in Holland and elsewhere was added an unparalleled gesture: theologians representing virtually every theological faculty and department in England and Scotland joined in a letter of protest to *The Times*. Because over approximately the same period the German theologian Hans Küng had also been involved in ongoing controversy with the church, Küng and Schillebeeckx came to be linked together as a pair of rebels allied in combatting the oppression of the Vatican (p. 2).

Nonetheless, Bowden continues, 'despite the problems they present – and they are very real ones – Schillebeeckx's books are a unique contribution to modern theology, and not only for his fellow Catholics. His name deserves to stand alongside that of Karl Barth, as being one of the very greatest theologians, not least – and this is the most important thing of all – in the sense of joy in believing which emerges so often in his theology . . .' (p. 3) 'Edward Schillebeeckx is . . . a Dominican whose love of the order is quite manifest . . . Worship is important for him . . . When asked by a journalist whether he talked with God, he

replied simply Yes, and when pressed to expand the monosyll-
able explained that he had never had any difficulty talking with
God as with a friend . . . 'You can only talk about God,' he
concluded, 'when you've been talking with him' (p. 6).

This fundamental emphasis on worship and on what can only
be described as liberating and liberated joy, on living human
experience of God, and on simplicity, should show us what
Schillebeeckx's theology is ultimately directed to and how he is
actually doing it. At best, Bowden says, it can be 'transcending
mere thinking in terms of rational concepts to provide a glimpse
of the glory of God, a glory which, however, can never be seen
unless it is set off against the history of human suffering and the
wretchedness of man that cries out for our efforts towards
liberation and relief and for God's new creation' (p. 19); it is
concerned with 'the salvation of humankind . . . making them
new men and women' (pp. ix.f.) from within a deeply-troubled
world and an equally troubled church which is unavoidably part
of it, reaching out for 'the transformation of the world . . .
(which) has been given over into the hands of contingent man;
(so that) he cannot expect God to relieve him of his problems . . .
Overcoming suffering and evil, wherever we may encounter
them, with all possible means of science and technology, with
the help of our fellow human beings, and if necessary by
revolution if nothing else will avail, is our task and our burden,
in a situation characterized by finitude and contingency.'[2]

There is so much in these quotations which really needs to be
spelt out. To break out of a Western, rationalized tradition of
Christian life shown up in the modern context as being sterile is
a first aim of Schillebeeckx. Next comes the recapturing of an
authentic living experience of the glory of God. But this glory is
to be no triumphalist, institutionalized one but one actually to
be found in the suffering and wretchedness of humankind. So a
further point is that the gospel, which was always about
salvation here and now, is to be rediscovered in the concrete
realities of today's world, this world and not some imagined
other. Since this has always been the locus of the gospel, in the
modern age which happens to be ours, science and technology
and all other so-called secular resources including, as we have
seen, if need be even revolution, are to be seen as gifts proper to

the task. The gospel then needs to be seen not merely as a message given 'once and for all', eternally calling humankind back to God and church in repentance, but as something fundamental indeed, which implies the transformation of the world and so must be bodied out in different forms at different points in human history. And Schillebeeckx's final aim here is restoration of a vision of utter humanness, a humanness which is enlarged, since it has to be forged in the heights and depths of triumph and tragedy, where all is simply 'finitude and contingency' which, being that, is both the glory of God and the glory of man simultaneously.

Of course behind these aims Schillebeeckx has at the centre of his mind those grass-roots communities of the Catholic church which have not been given full recognition, particularly those many 'basic' Third World ones struggling against injustice and oppression and for the concrete necessities of life. But those are also in turn the spur for the regeneration of church and theology and gospel as a whole. In that case transcendence is no longer to be located in an 'otherness' 'from above' focussed exclusively in the institution of the church. It is present absolutely, but now to be located in the world at large – and to be experienced there as something 'emptied': emptied of those secure things tradition-ally said by the church to be from above but, more than that, emptied in such a way that a fuller humanity is called out from within and realized more and more actually in 'self-emptying'. What may sound like no more than a clever word-play in fact 'conceals-reveals' a new spirituality, even mysticism, which is another of Schillebeeckx's major aims. It is a very human spirituality, appropriate to a modern world in which the traditional spirituality will no longer do, and is regularly described by Schillebeeckx as 'authentic creation faith'. It was supremely realized in Jesus, now no longer to be seen in the traditional forms of the triumphal Lord of the church and the cosmic Christ, but fundamentally as a man like us and particularly as true humanity, 'the man', who, 'emptied of divinity', was cast in the mould of servant of God and human kind, finally to become the suffering servant.[3]

It was by virtue of Jesus' faithfulness as this servant that God raised him up as an ultimate statement of the truth, and not through some indestructible power within. By this 'authentic creation faith', the so-called secular sphere and indeed the whole of the universe can be seen as thoroughly sacramental, and not just eschatological. Indeed in this light the concrete needs of Third World basic communities are no longer merely humanistic concerns, but sacramental signs of the meaning of things and the dignity of persons in God. By this 'authentic creation faith' Schillebeeckx breaks out of the dualistic two-world mentality of Moberly and Congar and truly establishes the one world of 'graced nature' which Congar was seeking after but could not achieve. The laity can therefore have that full position Congar was seeking for them, albeit now in a very different kind of church. 'Authentic creation faith' issues in 'a value, inspiration and orientation, which can constantly be universalized and in this sense secularized, which is to the advantage of all people and so as it were evades the monopoly or the particularity of the religions . . . On this basis, to the end of days finitude or secularity will continue to be directed towards the source and ground, inspiration and orientation, which transcends all secularity, which believers call the living God.'[4]

In this last quotation it is important to remember that Schillebeeckx is not looking solely upon creation in itself, but actually from the mind and heart of Jesus. But even if we recognize that, he still leaves us with real problems. For instance, has Christianity a distinctiveness, not to say uniqueness? Should secularity be given the meaning and the value which Schillebeeckx gives it? Is that not virtual atheism? What of church tradition and the institutions maintained as the true ones down so many centuries? Could those really have been so mistaken? If there is only one world now, indeed one process of human history, what 'certainties' and 'controlling points' can be left to us, who in that case are simply being swept along with the tide? What place for holiness is there in such a thoroughly ordinary life? Has not Schillebeeckx reduced theology to little more than evolutionism, to what Moberly and Congar saw as merely being 'from below'? Is not his theology too optimistic about human nature and the way life actually is in the real world? Has he not, like Moberly and Congar in their own ways, lost proper duality-within-unity in a reaction against the tradition, swinging the pendulum too far the other way? Is this not a new dualism, now separated off from God?

I believe that there is a satisfactory response to such problems, some of which are less serious than others. But because these problems are so significant for traditional theology and the traditional church, it is no wonder that Schillebeeckx has been treated as being beyond orthodoxy. However, there is something deeply authentic in his vision, in how, at the end of all things, indeed literally as the end of all creation, he sees not so much holiness as such but joy, joy which in its burning intensity is experienced as being indeed holy.

Such aims, directed ultimately towards this joy, not surprisingly match the way in which Schillebeeckx does theology. Bowden particularly observes how the reader must imagine Schillebeeckx as speaking, how he has admitted to beginning work without knowing precisely where it will end, how many brilliant judgments are often thrown out spontaneously in passing, how once a text is on a page it takes on a life which is its own; and also how Schillebeeckx will be so open to criticism that a second generation of writing will grow around the original, how the best way to describe his method is as being cumulative or 'in musical terms the extended language and loose structure of nineteenth-century romanticism rather than the ordered regularity of classical sonata form' (p. 17). Bowden uses Bruckner's breadth as a comparison. Such observations are hugely significant, pointing to the spirit of the man and his theology: human and bodily, open and investigative, responsible and spontaneous, humble before what truth is revealed, letting truth be done in dialogue, creative. They show Schillebeeckx's spirituality and its direction to be opposite to that of the tradition seen in Moberly and Congar. There, spirituality was centred upon what is inward and was directed towards what is above, beyond the ordinary and the human. Here, while spirituality certainly moves from the inward, it is continually reaching outwards into the ordinary and the human, and so in that very movement creating a fuller expression of humanity, Fixing on crucial words from this kind of theology, one can say that spirituality here is about living 'openly', 'riskily', 'by faith',

'in hope', 'vulnerably', finding life through death. It is not about
possessing or being possessed by God within, but actually
seeking and finding God in the depths and at the edges of
ordinary, human and secular experience and then through these
points looking to another kind of beyond in horizons of the
future.

   Schillebeeckx, then, does his theology by standing firmly in
the tradition, as in one sense he cannot but do, but looking
forward from it to concrete experienced realities in the present
in such a way that there is mutual interaction. Realities in the
present highlight points in the tradition; points in the tradition
highlight present realities. But the thrust of this mutual
interpretation or, as it has come to be called, hermeneutical
circle (although this does of course have its problems), is more
fundamental than perhaps it sounds. For the highlighting does
not lead Schillebeeckx back into tradition as it is convention-
ally understood, but to rework and reinterpret it, turning it to
see other aspects. Tradition is then seen as a living thing, not
fossilized; a body of actual living responses from real people to
their situations at their own points in the history of this one
world. But since, further, it is response, as distinct from mere
transmission, the highlighting is actually a process of comparison and contrast, of dialogue between points in history, out of
which response is elicited in the present, 'when God speaks'.
Nor is such a response solely for the present, but also in its very
nature for the future. For while it must affirm present realities,
in so doing it sees in them prefigurements of the ends for which
they are made and therefore looks forward to their consummation. All this amounts to a process of creative dialogue, dialogue
between different points in history seen to be one history of
salvation. And it is of course when we turn to the church and its
self-understanding and theology that we find this process at its
most intense.

Schillebeeckx has written two books about ministry. The
first, *Ministry. A Case for Change*, was written in 1980 and
first published in English in 1981. This caused a considerable
stir and provoked a number of criticisms, some of which
seemed entirely to have missed the point of the book and

which Schillebeeckx felt to be misinterpretations. So he re-wrote *Ministry*. The second version was published in both its Dutch and English versions in 1985, under the English title *The Church with a Human Face. A New and Expanded Theology of Ministry.* The later version did not substantially alter the approach of the earlier one; however, Schillebeeckx did make his treatment of the historical evidence on which he based his case much more comprehensive and detailed, and removed or substantiated at length some of the more sweeping generalizations which had been so vulnerable to attack.[5]

'The critical point – in every sense of the phrase – is whether the practice of the ministry . . . is shaped primarily by theolog-ical criteria or on the basis of non-theological factors. Or, more precisely, whether it is formed from theological reflection on new human and cultural situations' (*Ministry*, p. 2). The standpoint and the assumptions could not be clearer, in the light of what has already been said. Schillebeeckx is also specifically aware of the situation set out in Kerkhofs' statistics which we noted in Chapter 2.[6] 'If, sociologically speaking, there seems to be such a shortage of priests, something has gone wrong with the way in which believers look at their church and those who hold office in it (and with the way in which they put their views into practice)' (*Ministry*, p. 1). Criticism of any institution is, of course, always directed primarily at the leadership, and in a sharply double-edged quotation from Jerome, with which he opens his work, Schillebeeckx lays the ground for his own: 'There can be no church community without a leader or team of leaders' (*Ministry*, p. 1).

That sounds reasonable enough, the ordinary person might think. But the question is the way in which 'community' is understood. For the church community which Schillebeeckx has in mind is not the great Catholic church world-wide, nor a great diocese with its bishop, but the local church, particularly the grass-roots Christians without a priest who, lacking the 'eucharistic principle', cannot in Congar's terms be seen as 'completing the true apostolic work', even though they are making new disciples and building up the gospel. One of these communities is much smaller than the traditional church institution; it is probably cell-like, distinctly human, centred in the world in ordinary experience here and now, and may well be exclusively lay. Like any group, this community will throw up its own leadership, but this will be 'from below'. Schillebeeckx argues that what will naturally happen in this way should be recognized in such communities as true priesthood or ordained ministry; at the same time, too, such communities ought naturally to be entitled to celebrate the eucharist and all in all be regarded as fully legitimate. For such leadership as is thrown up is not *just* the natural phenomenon to be seen in any group, but actually its expression within the group living specifically in the spirit of Jesus.

What more is needed? The similarity with all other groups is a significant reminder of the closeness of grace and nature here! Furthermore, if such communities and such priesthood or ordained ministry significantly differ from what they are in other parts of the worldwide church, that should lead us to a renewed understanding of the church and its catholicity: it is now no longer hierarchical, imperial, but a community of communities 'in collegiality' embracing diverse expressions of Christian life. In fact, on the strength of new biblical scholarship, not available to Moberly and scarcely seen by Congar, Schillebeeckx is able to claim that this was the original understanding throughout the New Testament period and more or less over the first Christian millennium. What is ultimately implied here is no mere call for tolerance, but a challenge to the very heart of the tradition which has developed, to understandings of priesthood or ordained ministry, church and theology as a whole. Effectively reviving an old argument put forward by Hatch, Lightfoot and Hort against Moberly, Schillebeeckx implies that what is said to be 'from above' has always only been 'from below'. To say this can never be to reduce Christian life to *mere* secularity, since the gospel of the kingdom of God has broken into human history and the history of the world. It is, however, to say that Christian life has ever since been a potential at grass roots. What has in fact happened is that what has always been, in this sense, 'from below', has become wrongly institutionalized, separated from the grass roots in another world which is said to be 'from above'. The separation between priesthood and lay people is therefore a false one, which cannot be found in the earlier history of the church. It is therefore also wrong to have a separated theology and spirituality.

For those committed to the tradition as it has come to be understood, all this, of course, has been anathema. To a Polish model of ministry in which the church has traditionally been strong, and must be strong as an institution in the face of atheistic communism, this must seem to be dangerously close to atheism, particularly where Marxist models of understanding social and political situations are openly acknowledged. So Schillebeeckx has been accused of simply rewriting history with an eye to present-day problems, a charge which he firmly rebutted.[6] The argument is so fierce because behind these two polarized positions is the question of what Christian life and spirit truly is. Is it to do with 'otherness' and a 'beyond' which is to be located exclusively in the church as an institution? Is it to do with the kind of holiness which that kind of institution has undoubtedly created? Or is it to do with another kind of 'otherness' which certainly has its 'beyond', but which is to be found primarily in the depths of humanness and 'within' human situations? Is it to do with another kind of holiness which can be found, for instance, in wretchedness and suffering, and in the joy which pours out in genuine liberation? Of course Schillebeeckx is writing from the latter position, and his vision and theology certainly aim at a major reformation for the whole of the church.

Like Luther nearly five hundred years before, he turns to the New Testament to begin his argument, reviving the notorious issue of the relationship between scripture and church tradition. Which is to be primary when they seem to be in conflict? The disunity of the churches shows continuing disagreement about the answers, which becomes more intense, the more fundamentalist the presuppositions being held. Drawing above all on new biblical scholarship and his own sense of history, however, Schillebeeckx transcends the simplistic dichotomy by articulating the existential dimension to both these things, thus bringing them together in one historical continuum.

With a deep insight, which is reflected in other of his works,[7]

Schillebeeckx entitled the first chapter of his original book 'The *Story* of New Testament Communities'. By using the term story, he is moving from 'objective' history to focus on the experience of real people in their here and now, of which the New Testament is variously the story. This is a significant shift, recalling the spirit in the man and his conflict with the authorities in his church. For it calls for gifts of imagination and intuition as well as of intellect, and for deep understanding of sheer humanity and the business of existence. It calls for perception and recognition, rather than rationality. This produces greater reality and better theology. Schillebeeckx recovers the belief that people and their experience of existence are fundamentally the same throughout history. This enables people in the present to see their own experience through the patterns of the past, so that their feel for God here and now must inevitably be sharpened, so that they too are given a sense of belonging to a particular people in a particular process in history.

Fundamentalist understandings of Bible and church tradition, so prone to wrong idealism, are brought down properly to earth. People can thus be freed from destructive beliefs about some golden age in the past from which we have irredeemably fallen – meaning that we need to remain within a church-world for our salvation, and keep ourselves untainted. Every human endeavour is doomed to failure from the start, in that we do not in fact take on the full responsibility which is properly ours and do not properly believe in ourselves. In Schillebeeckx's approach, based on the concept of story, Bible and church tradition are just as authoritative, but in a new sense of being 'authentic' and 'normative'. This implies that the church experienced by succeeding generations, of which they variously told the story, is true not because it is Bible or church tradition but because it has the ring of truth; that this truth, too, is gathered 'normatively', but not literalistically, to provide keys to unlock our own present in our own way. Of course, as we have already recognized, there is inevitably a weakness in such a historical method in that there are no 'outside' reference points from which to judge. Judgment can only be 'from within', finding points of reference within the common history from what is authentic in the present, and from a vision of consummation in the future. But this is the unavoidable consequence of this kind of theology, and it is by no means as uncertain as it may sound.

When Schillebeeckx discusses the New Testament period, in line with modern scholarship, he begins with the pattern of Jesus and his 'messianic' communities, bringing out the very different picture of Jesus and his intentions which has now come to be accepted throughout Gospel studies. He then turns to what he calls the 'early communities of Christian believers', dividing their history into two phases: the first generation, followed by the post-apostolic period. In the former, 'Apart from apostleship proper, the Christian communities did not receive any kind of church order from the hands of Jesus when he still shared our earthly history. Furthermore, the Twelve were the symbol of the approaching eschatological community of God, which originally was not yet organized for a long-term earthly history' (*Church with a Human Face*, p. 74). There was simply a consciousness of being sent. Order was a spirit which would subsequently inform all that would have to happen. So: 'Since according to the self-understanding of the first Christians the Christian community is a community of God, a community of Christ and a temple of the Holy Spirit, it is obvious that what developed spontaneously from the community of faith (as we would now put it, in accordance with the sociological laws of group formation), was rightly and spontaneously experienced by the communities as a "gift of the Lord". The New Testament, bubbling over with praise for "blessings from above", does not know the later contrast between what comes "from below" and what comes "from above"' (p. 74). The daring reference to sociological laws emphasizes how Spirit is not inward, as with Moberly and Congar, but to be found at the points where the gospel intersects with the world and creates Christian community. It also signals the closure of the gap between two separated worlds of grace and nature (across which an interventionist God is seen to perform miracles from one into the other), to be replaced by one world of graced nature. But as I have already pointed out, this by no means leads to mere secularity.

Schillebeeckx also points out that while the Twelve

undoubtedly form a nucleus, apostleship clearly extends beyond them and is very fluid at the periphery. Paul most obviously breaks the mould. New Testament evidence is adamant that his apostleship was in no way transmitted by the Twelve, but it was recognized *de facto*. Paul himself also refers to apostles who experienced the risen Christ other than Peter, the Twelve and James. Then, too, there were the many called apostles and prophets who were constantly on the move, later said to be the foundation of the first communities. These first communities received the faith from these apostles on the basis of the personal experiences that most of them had had of Jesus, but it is a significant feature of the concept of apostleship that such experiences were not thought to have been transmissible. For Schillebeeckx, concerned for a living, fully-incarnated experience rather than a transmitted teaching in company with a transmitted ontological order, this latter point is crucial.

So what were apostleship and apostolicity in this first phase? They were both to do with the church, the communities, as a whole. Where the spreading gospel was found to intersect with the world and build up communities from the grass roots, those communities were themselves apostolic, since they were founded upon the apostolic Gospel. While focus upon particular persons such as Peter and Paul in the developing church was obviously necessary, the church was by no means hierarchical. So Paul's obvious position as founder of the community and references to Timothy, often said to show marks of apostolic succession, are to be understood within the fundamental reality of community. The fact that apostleship can be seen at this period to have been very fluid and that names for ministries are in no way fixed is not to be taken to mean that the church had yet to formalize its order from the centre. Rather, they are indications of what is to be expected from an 'irruptive gospel', how many different forms of life and leadership were thrown up as the Spirit took root in this culture and that. So church communities were locally inspired, from the grass roots, in response to the gospel. They held together as a community of communities, pointing forward to the eschatological communality of all things. Leadership was locally inspired, as one gift of the Spirit among many in a gift-orientated community. Service was the basic model of the common life, of one another and God, following Jesus the servant. Apostolicity was therefore none other than the foundation upon which the communities themselves had come to stand, the gospel as it had taken root in their particular context. All in all, in this first phase discipleship rather than apostleship is the dominant feature, quite contrary to the picture painted by Moberly and Congar.

In the second phase, between roughly AD 80 and AD 100, and after the first generation had died, above all including the apostles and prophets (and with them the expectation of the Second Coming had also died), ministry began to take on specific forms, though these still continued to change. Even so, Schillebeeckx remarks, 'people were less interested in actual structures of ministry or in uniform titles for ministers' (p. 81). Again in the light of modern biblical scholarship, he acceptably divides the New Testament evidence into a series of areas, with the effect of again depicting a community of communities, local churches pursuing the practice of ministry in their own contexts. Apostolicity is again localized, a matter of discipleship. In one area evidenced by the letter to the Ephesians, which Schillebeeckx rightly assumes to be pseudonymous and post- Pauline, there is admittedly a first sign of institutionalizing, probably presbyteral, and leadership must now be responsible to the apostolic heritage. But what does this amount to? It is 'a reference to original experiences of real people who had arrived at a surprising new life through their encounter with Jesus . . . apostolicity points among other things to the distinguishing mark of the community as being discipleship of Jesus in teaching and life-style' (p. 83). Leadership, 'now the church's ministry – is thus experienced as a special ministerial charisma in the service of the community, as the transformation into a specific specialist ministry of what is the task of everyone who is "baptized in the Spirit"' (p. 83).

In the churches of the Pastoral Epistles, I Peter and James, 'Primarily the concern is quite definitely not so much with an unbroken succession or continuity in the ministry as with an unbroken succession in teaching, in the apostolic tradition . . .

This is expressed even in the rite of the laying on of hands, which these letters want to see introduced and which is already beginning to become a tradition in these churches. For here, too, there is primarily no question of the transference of ministerial authority, but of the charisma of the Holy Spirit, which will help the minister to hand down and preserve in a living way the pledge entrusted to him and to make him able to proclaim the apostolic tradition intact' (p. 101). And if we ask what ministries are needed: 'specific form is . . . evidently a pastoral question, which the church must consider afresh on each occasion' (p. 102). Schillebeeckx demonstrates that other areas are similar. Moreover, throughout both these phases of the early church: 'one striking fact is that the ministry did not develop from and around the eucharist or the liturgy, but from the apostolic building up of the community through preaching, admonition and leadership. No matter what different forms it takes, ministry is concerned with the leadership of the community: ministers are pioneers, those who inspire the community and serve as models by which the whole community can identify the gospel' (p. 119). There is 'evidently no special problem as to who should preside at the eucharist . . .' In a position which is a complete *volte face* from Moberly and Congar, Schillebeeckx argues that eucharist is to serve discipleship, in the sense of the community's proclamation of the gospel of the kingdom in the world and human history, and the continuing upbuilding of it as its sign and sacrament; the discipleship is not in the service of the eucharist, and all that that has come to stand for. 'There are no biblical grounds anywhere for a sacral and mystical foundation to the ministry in the eucharist. If we remember that the early eucharist was structured after the pattern of Jewish grace at meals . . . at which not just anyone could preside, it is evident that the leaders of house communities *ipso facto* also presided at the eucharist, and this is also evident from the texts written at the same time as the last part of the New Testament' (pp. 119f.).

In *Ministry* Schillebeeckx had spoken even more strongly: 'The eucharist is Jesus' parting gift to the whole community, which therefore has a right to it – the right by grace – regardless of all kinds of complicated problems over the ministry' (p. 30). He went on to conclude: 'The community has a right to a minister or ministers and to the celebration of the eucharist. This apostolic right has priority over criteria for admission which the church can and may impose on its ministers' (p. 37). The understanding of apostolicity and church on which these stunning claims are based could not be more radically challenging for the church as we have come to know it.

There is no space here to go in detail into the shift which took place between this earliest understanding of Christian community and the nature of ministry within it, and the view which has become established today, particularly within the Roman Catholic Church. Schillebeeckx painted it in broad brush strokes in *Ministry* and then described it in much more detail in *The Church with a Human Face*, taking the wind out of the sails of those of his critics who accused him of oversimplification: the brush strokes may have been too sweeping in the first instance, but the picture proved to be essentially the same in the end. To see the point Schillebeeckx is making, there is no substitute for reading the original.

To those who have done precisely that, what he has demonstrated beyond doubt is the changing character of ministry and church down Christian history. But his work goes far deeper than this. It shows that the understanding of ministry and church which is so often taken for granted and the direction in which they are traditionally focussed are fundamentally untrue to the gospel, at least in our present context. At the very least, in the present context of a world shackled, suffering and crying out for liberation and joy, it is the case that priesthood or ordained ministry, church and the theology which supports all these, cannot rightly be located in a separated institution 'from above'. All these are in fact to be seen in terms of the fundamental belief that in the human Jesus the gospel climactically broke out into human history and the history of the world, as a fact never to be undone. It is now within our tradition, in this sense of the word, for ever. It is God's ultimate word in history, but with the potential to reach out to the ends of the earth and the end of history. Where it intersects with the world, the kingdom is discovered, in the depths and at the edges of ordinary experience, and church communities are naturally built up, for this is the very nature of the gospel. In their humanness, these communities are sacraments of the Spirit and signs of ultimate consummation in the communality of all things. They are also the continuing servants of God and the gospel. But all this demands that the gospel as message, that church structures, should not in any way be fixed, but that the gospel should be bodied out uniquely as a response to each new, succeeding concrete agenda, from within each new, succeeding concrete context. The term 'succeeding' deliberately implies a process which continually reaches out; therefore in and through the concrete church it must arise from the grass roots, from the community of communities in which the gospel actually takes root. And theology must be by praxis: experience first and reflection upon it afterwards. In that case authority is not 'from above', but from within the communities themselves in their contexts and their reciprocal dialogue. Ministry, seen to be far wider than traditional priesthood or ordained ministry, and church structure and theology as a whole, are in that case matters of pastoral practicality.

On this fundamentally different basis from that understood by Moberly and Congar, lay people at last receive the fullness of status that they could not be given earlier. On this basis there can at last be genuine spirituality and a theology of the laity. Spirituality and theology as a whole have their perspective and presupposition fundamentally shifted, to the one world at large and the forward perspective of its history. On this fundamentally different basis the facts and problems of Chapter 2 can all at last be genuinely engaged from within and will be seen to contain open possibilities, to be decided on by individual church communities, perhaps prefiguring the coming of a new church.

However, there may be criticism here. Does not all this imply mere reductionism to the simply human, reductionism of the transcendent to the relational, virtual atheism? But as we shall see in the next chapter, this is the thinking of the 'essentialist' tradition. By contrast, Schillebeeckx has recast Christian faith and life within an existentialist tradition, which is just as respectable, and infinitely more appropriate to modern times with demands which must not and cannot be ignored if human history and the church within it are to undergo an authentic revival.

Fourth Interlude

Three passions, simple but overwhelmingly strong, have gov-
erned my life: the longing for love, the search for knowledge and
unbearable pity for the suffering of mankind. These passions,
like great winds, have blown me hither and thither, in a
wayward course, over a deep ocean of anguish, reaching to the
very verge of despair . . . Love and knowledge, so far as they were
possible, led upwards towards the heavens. But always pity
brought me back to earth. Echoes of cries of pain reverberate in
my heart. Children in famine, victims tortured by oppressors,
helpless old people a burden to their sons, and the whole world
of loneliness, poverty and pain made a mockery of what human
life should be. I long to alleviate the evil, but I cannot, and I too
suffer.

Bertrand Russell[1]

One of my early loves in the world of philosophy was Maritain.
Years ago he seemed to be asking questions which were so
fundamental to life, and in recent days I have been re-reading his
work. It has not been an idle reading. He has been one of the
many authors I have gone to for help in an effort to reflect upon
my life in the Inner City. He has not offered me solutions or hard
certitudes, but one passage has assisted me in attempting to
formulate or clarify the issues which I have already raised in
these pages: the issues about the church and the human, the loss
of the ascetic, and the real issues which priesthood and the
religious life must face for radicalization. The passage seminally

articulates what I wish to say about my experience in the Inner City of Liverpool. I quote the passage in full:

'Whenever we have to deal with the ingredients of human history, we are prone to consider matters from the point of view of action or of ideas which shape action. Yet it is necessary to consider them also – and primarily – from the point of view of existence. I mean there is another, and more fundamental, order than that of social and political action; it is the order of communion in life, desire and suffering. In other words there must be recognized the category to exist with and suffer with.

To act for belongs to the realm of benevolence. To exist with and to suffer with, to the realms of love in unity. Love is given to an existing, concrete being . . . The one I love, I love him right or wrong; and I wish to exist and suffer with him.

To exist with is an ethical category. It does not mean to live with someone in a physical sense, or in the same way as he does; and it does not mean loving someone in the sense of wishing him well; it means loving someone in the sense of becoming one with him, of bearing his burdens, of living a common moral life with him, of feeling with him and suffering with him.

If one loves that human thing which is called "the people" and which, like all human and living things, is, I know, very difficult to define, but all the more real, then one's first and basic wish will be to exist, to stay in communion with the people.

Before doing them good, or working for their good, before following or rejecting the political line of this or that group, which claims to be supporting their interests, before weighing conscientiously the good and evil to be expected from the doctrines and historical trends which ask for their support and choosing amongst them, or in certain exceptional cases, rejecting them all, before doing any of these things, one will have chosen to exist with the people, to assume the people's hardships and destiny.'

Austin Smith[2]

CHAPTER SIX

Towards New Ministry, Priesthood and Church

In the Church of England General Synod in February 1984, the Tiller strategy, which we considered in Chapter 2, was debated; subsequently, specific questions were referred to dioceses and deaneries for a response. This was an example of what I feel to be the rightful government of the church's life and pastoral task, by lay people as well as clergy. However, not surprisingly, given what we have seen in the three previous chapters, there was ambiguity over these questions. It arose on the one hand out of a desire to recognize full status for lay people and a desire for 'mission', and yet on the other from a belief that the reality of ministry is fundamentally 'from above', and exclusively located in the institution of the church, essentially in priesthood or ordained ministry. One question asked was whether 'shared ministry', embracing laity as well as clergy, should be developed for the future, involving corporate leadership 'at every level', and recognizing the gifts of every baptized member, but it really begged the question of the extent and kind of sharing that was possible, particularly with its talk of levels. The basic question underlying all this emerged very quickly: should a strong stipendiary ordained ministry continue to be an important element in the church's ministry?

Another question asked was whether the stipendiary ministry, ordained and lay, should be fully deployed for the priorities of mission, but begged the further issue of what mission actually is, an issue brought into special focus in the fact that this ministry was seen as being both ordained and lay. This sharper focus is not always evident, since the lay ministry is trained along the same lines as the ordained, and is therefore often seen as a mere extension or pale reflection of it. A fourth question was whether further development of the non-stipendiary ministry, which has been so much more evident in recent times, should be welcomed: after all, it is still uncertain in shape and vocation, and holds together both the traditional idea of ordained ministry and that of an authorized Christian presence in secular spheres, like places of work. But the further question was again begged as to what this ministry, already so packed with tension, would be developed into.

Perhaps the issue of this ministry focussed more sharply than any of the other issues the ambiguity that was present with them all. At a point of encounter between Christian gospel and ordinary life which, say at places of work, could hardly be much more radical, how should this ministry come to be seen? As a holy presence 'sent' to the secular world of work from fundamentally the base of traditional ordained ministry, and so merely an extension of it and with nothing much more to say or do except to 'witness quietly'? Or as the presence of someone who seeks to body out the gospel afresh from within specific, concrete and continually new contexts, bringing his or her praxis to bear on the theological tradition of the church? What interpretation should be made of the situation and experience of the non-stipendiary minister? More importantly, who actually should be making it, and what is the starting point for interpretation? What training should be given?

It was in connection with questions like this, with massive unrecognized and unexamined presuppositions, that the main question about the development of ministry was put. Significantly, General Synod finally called for a development of adult education programmes for all those who responded to shared ministry, but by the same token as before, the question was again begged as what the focus of such programmes would be. In short, the model of ministry and therefore of the church which underlay all the Synod's questions was precisely the institutional one we noted with Moberly and, most frustratingly, with Congar. Lay people, it was hoped, would become more prominent in the church, but in what sense would they be able to 'share' in ministry? Would they not actually prove to be mere extensions, pale reflections, of a traditional clericalized ministry? Indeed, does this not already happen when questions like those put by General Synod are framed and responded to, in that laity readily concede their own distinctiveness and particularly their immediate experience of what mission and ministry might mean in the modern secular world, looking to the clergy for guidance in such 'theological matters'. And the clergy usually already assume that they know what the theology 'is', since they 'have been trained in it'. I myself value my original theological training very highly, but I have to admit that it gave me little, if any, opportunity to recognize the perspectives raised in this book, and I believe that most clergy would have to say the same thing.

The basic problem is that Tiller's *Strategy*, and all the other facts and problems which we considered in Chapter 2, as by no means isolated issues, have come into being in an in-between time, when two diametrically opposed views of life and of faith are in existence and indeed in conflict. The existence of these opposing views, as I have pointed out, largely goes unrecognized and unexamined. But an understanding of them is essential if we are to make any progress. The main characteristics of each opposing view have already been pointed out in the previous chapters, but to make things quite clear I shall now set them out in schematic form:

	Essentialist	Existentialist (or Historical)
Centres of interest	There-and-then	Here-and-now
	Out there/up there/ beyond the stars/over the rainbow/above-beyond	Down in the depths/ in the ground of being/ within/ultimate reality
	Otherness	The human and the secular
	Ideals and dreams	Reality, truth and meaning
. . . sought through	Ideas and propositions	Experience and awareness
	Objectivity	Subjectivity/ contextuality

	Essentialist	Existentialist (or Historical)
. . . and corruptions in	Idealism/idolatry	Humanism
	Mind-matter dualism/gnosticism	Materialism
	Rational reductionism	Nihilism
Character of theology	Nature and essence of things/ontological	Fact and existence of things/contextual-relational/functional
	Abstract	Concrete
	Eternal	Historical
	Heavenly-spiritual	Incarnational
	Uniform	Plural
	Rational	Experiential
	Deductive	Inductive
Character of spirituality	Other worldly/separated from fallen world	This-worldly/redeemed yet sinful
	Invisible and inward	Visible and outward
	Individualized and private	Communal-personal/socio-political
	Sacred	Human
	Holiness	Wholeness
	Law	Love
	Living through believing	Living through dying
Characters and images of God . . .	Transcendent	Immanent
	Father	Spirit
	Lord/king/law giver/judge/shepherd/leader/master/Holy One	Redeemer/reconciler/lover/Merciful One/
		God-with-us
	More masculine	More feminine
. . . of Jesus Christ	Christ the Lord	Jesus the Man
	Triumphal Lord of Church	Self-emptying suffering servant in the world/Man for others
	Enthroned in highest heaven	Crucified God/Lamb of God
Character of Church . . .	Institutional/structured	Communal/personal
	Centralized/hierarchical/uniform	Decentralized/grass-roots/diversified
	Status	Function
	Authoritative by teaching	Authoritative by serving

	Essentialist	Existentialist (or Historical)
	Clerical	Human/charismatic
	From above	From below
	Exclusive	Inclusive/ecumenical
. . . and images	Body of Christ	People of God
	Ark of Salvation/Mother Church/Feeder of the Faithful/Sheepfold	Suffering Servant
	Oracle of God	Herald of Salvation
	True Church	Sacrament and Sign of God in the world/ Outcrop of God

Now this schema certainly needs to be approached with care. For instance, if theology in the essentialist approach is said to be abstract and rational while in the existentialist approach it is said to be concrete and experiential, this should not be understood to mean that the former is devoid of experience of any kind or the latter of abstraction and rationality. After all, who can pick ideas out of the air? Who can experience anything without ideas, which are essential to the very business of experiencing? So too, if spirituality in the essentialist approach is said to be invisible, individual and characterized by law while in the existentialist approach it is visible, communal and characterized by love, this should not be understood to mean that the former is without what the latter is and has or vice versa. Again, if God in the essentialist approach is imaged as Father while in the existentialist position God is imaged as Spirit, this should not be understood to mean that the former approach is not concerned for God as Spirit or the latter for God as Father. The crucial thing is the fundamental core on each side, from which all such forms, expressions and images come. That core will determine the precise meaning of such terms as abstraction and experience, invisibility and visibility, law and love, Father and Spirit. So we cannot merely read off individuals and groups from the schema at face value. For all that, even so, there are two diametrically opposite views. So in the essentialist approach, for example, Father and Spirit, law, and so on will be more distant and other, while in the existentialist approach they will be closer and more human.

The essentialist approach is, of course, that of Moberly and Congar. With them it was certainly human and personal in its own way, with Congar longing to break the mould and to get into ordinary human experience. But that proved impossible because of a whole body of presuppositions which we can now see represented in the left hand column of the schema. In fact because of the unrecognized influence of idealism, all these categories are taken way beyond the concerns of ordinary human existence. And the influence of this approach still exists today, making for the same problems. The existentialist approach is that taken by Schillebeeckx, and the thrust of it in our time, particularly with the facts and problems of Chapter 2 in mind, is very penetrating.

For one thing, proceeding on the tacit assumption that all truth is held together within a duality-in-unity, it asks whether we can properly speak of 'cores' on each side, or indeed of two positions at all. And if there should be only one position, with both sides perhaps holding together in tension across a centre in the crucible, which side actually leads in interpretation? Where should the starting point be?

This latter question is a crucial one, which I have already referred to in connection with the problem for the existentialist approach posed by the hermeneutical circle. But that problem can also be found in the essentialist approach. The existentialist approach, where experience is thought to be a prior necessity, to be followed by reflection in the light of tradition before a return to experience in a deepened and confirmed reading of it, and so on, obviously has to face the problem whether all this is not mere subjective selection. Schillebeeckx's historical method, the model of his theology, has this fundamental problem, causing him to be accused of merely rewriting history with an eye to solving present-day problems. His response was to say that we cannot but be subjective, since we are an integral part of our own context and cannot significantly step outside it. 'For me the method followed is the only reason why history is worth the difficulties of reading it; tradition becomes a living tradition because facts that had been forgotten can again be called to mind, expounded and interpreted. We cannot cross out our own present, push it on one side or disregard it. Anyone who believes that is wrong, in supposing such a thing is possible . . . Consciously or unconsciously, people look at historical documents in the light of present-day questions, suppositions and hypotheses, and above all in the light of "negative experiences". The critical problem is whether one simply looks to history to confirm one's own already established views or whether one allows them to be put to the test by history.'[1]

But the essentialist position equally cannot avoid a similar charge of eclectic subjectivism, and being involved in the fundamental problem of a hermeneutical circle. For it too must be automatically interpreting experience, and by applying objective truths must inevitably be making for experience in an already determined form, which is then seen to confirm the tradition. 'Signs following' have thus often been traditionally said to be the confirmation which is to be sought. But are these not equally no more than an integral part of our context, seen from the beginning in a particular perspective?

The truth is that both essentialist and existentialist positions equally are involved in a hermeneutical problem, beginning with the crucial question of a starting point. And if that is the case, which should be prior in interpretation, in search of a centre in the duality-within-unity?

There can surely be only one convincing answer: the existentialist approach. The essentialist approach simply does not meet the modern situation. It leaves the church locked up in itself, getting more and more fossilized by the minute, with the world left to its own devices. It cannot find any common point of concern with the humanizing revolution running through this period of human history. It cannot cope with the facts and problems of Chapter 2. Moreover, as Schillebeeckx has made clear, it is by no means the sole position which has been adopted in Christian history. The church has never been 'eternal', but always historical. The claim of being eternal reflects only the desire of the church to live above and beyond the world in a particular period of its history. Furthermore, while the essentialist approach has assuredly led to holiness, we may well ask just what this 'holiness' is that it has produced. Indeed, is 'holiness' an expression of the gospel? Is not the kind of language which Schillebeeckx uses more appropriate for our day? For here is talk of a genuine liberation and joy, ultimately for a world created and loved by God, not without genuine threat and the pain of separation, but no longer hidden away and avoided in an institutionalized separation. So this genuine liberation and joy also carries with it a genuine potential for paying a price, which can even be martyrdom. Is there not here a renewal of the vision of Paul, of *koinonia*, of the rich mystery of humanity in Christ, the deepest union in the communality of all, where God, the ground of all, will be all in all.

And here the church, as human community, is called to be the living sign and sacrament of the *koinonia*, and the servant, a suffering servant, of the proclamation of its presence in the world and the process of human history. If we move from a prophetic vision like this back to the problems with which we began, we can see them now as issues also of genuine and theologically proper possibility in which breakthrough into fundamental renewal can be achieved, in what I believe to be truly a historic moment.

Crisis of identity

'For many who are in positions of isolation, the old clerical piety, which accepted loneliness as part of the priestly vocation, no longer consoles. For theirs is not the loneliness of the pioneer apostle but the isolation of those who sense that they are being squeezed out of society, which . . . includes them in the same category as other antique and picturesque functionaries left over from a former age.'

Since these words of Victor de Waal's, which we have already come across,[2] were written in 1969, efforts have been made in a good many places to change the situation: in liturgical renewal, in re-emphasizing the place of lay people in the church, in pioneering new forms of ministry, in openness to new spiritual dynamic. But on the whole it has to be admitted that the situation nevertheless remains fundamentally unaltered, partly because of the natural resistance to such things, but basically because what has been needed has been a new theology, taking in every fundamental of the Christian faith, without which what has been done cannot have gone nearly far enough.

So on top of the burdens normally to be expected in the ministry the clergyman – and his family – have had to carry the burden of an old vision in a new time, and this has inevitably sapped the heart of his belief and his integrity. Any clergyman alive to the modern situation ought to be aware of the cost in personal terms; but there are those who are not, and as colleagues these also prove to be an added burden.

That this crisis of identity is indeed one involving great personal cost and is not just an academic question is evident from two major books describing the struggle with it. One, W. H. Vanstone's *Love's Endeavour, Love's Expense*, published by Darton, Longman and Todd in 1977, was by a Church of England parish priest who endeavoured to break the mould through total loving self-sacrifice; the other, Austin Smith, *Passion for the Inner City*, published by Sheed and Ward in 1983, was the story of a Catholic Passionist monk frozen in traditional monastic spirituality and life who more radically came to break the mould by moving to an utterly human frontier in Liverpool's inner city. Both books spoke of renewal from the existential dimension, from fundamental experience in the modern world. For in words of Harry Williams in a Foreword to the former, though they apply equally to both: 'Theological truth is the truth of God's relationship with man and it is the fruit not of learning but of experience. In this sense all theology, properly so called, is written in blood. It is an attempt to communicate what has been discovered at great cost in the deepest places of the heart – by sorrow and joy, frustration and fulfilment, defeat and victory, agony and ecstasy, tragedy and triumph. Theology, properly so called, is the record of a man's wrestling with God. Wounded in some way or other by the struggle the man will certainly be, but in the end he will obtain the blessing promised to those who endure. The theologian in this respect is no different from the poet or dramatist. All of them must write in blood' (p. xi). This reflection or renewal from the existential side is a particularly important one, for if the leadership of the church has previously been schooled above all in what I have called the essentialist tradition and has had little opportunity for fundamental experience in the modern world since, how else is genuine renewal to take place?

This essentialist tradition as represented by Moberly and Congar has responded to the current crisis of identity by calls for renewal and revival. Like the birth of the Oxford Movement at a time of similar crisis in 1833, in the Church of England there has been a strong call for 'Catholic renewal', for reaffirmation of 'the true Catholic faith' and its 'true priesthood'. Similarly, on the Evangelical side there has been a strong concern for 'church growth' and for evangelistic revival, under such figures as Billy Graham and Luis Palau. For both sides of this tradition renewal and revival have, of course, been in terms of 'otherness' and that kind of holiness, and against what has pejoratively been described as secular society. Here concern for the role of the ordained ministry has been ultimately unimportant. For as we have seen, in this approach the ordained ministry is not ultimately about function at all, or about relationship. It is not ultimately 'for' anything, but 'is as it is'. It is a matter of 'status', whether this is 'indelibly imprinted within', as in the Catholic understanding, or a 'call from the Lord' as in the Evangelical. On this understanding it has been almost inevitable that the response to the identity crisis has been to go further 'within', into those things which 'are as they are', which are 'given'. For there is a sense in which the church in the essentialist tradition cannot *fundamentally* relate to the world around it; is not *fundamentally* related to so-called secular society.

Interestingly, the crisis of identity and the problem of isolation have called forth from Catholic priests a response which powerfully symbolizes the essentialist dilemma. This is the modern practice of priests concelebrating at the eucharist, all reciting the words of consecration together. For this practice expresses the modern quest for community and no doubt provides personal comfort at times of identity crisis. But community here goes only so far as the altar rail and cannot properly include lay people, let alone anything fundamental from the so-called secular world. The focus for community is in fact 'otherness', and the fact that this must mean personal and private individuation is reflected precisely in the fact that each priest has to recite the words of consecration. This does not, then, actually express community, but is a classic compromise response to the essentialist dilemma in modern times, that of the relationship between otherness and human community. It is a living symbol, before our eyes, of the problem of maintaining proper duality-within-unity and of the ever-present danger of declining into dualism.

The existentialist tradition, represented by Schillebeeckx, offers quite another possibility. Here the gospel has not just been given to the church, but is seen, as in the New Testament, as having at last broken into human history, as a fact never to be undone. It therefore continues to be a living reality within the world at large. Here is no 'essentially and eternally unchanging message' but an 'embodiment' to be discovered continually afresh in the process of human history, in response to the world's agenda. With this picture the priest or minister (and by implication all others with him), can indeed recover his identity, through his fundamental calling to be one who proclaims the presence of the kingdom here and now and so as a pioneer and upbuilder of community. Here he simultaneously takes up the process of salvation history set going by Jesus himself and won at great cost. By definition, this gospel demands no clergyman, no church, disembodied or institutionally separated or six feet above criticism, but utter commitment with people in the market place and indeed at every corner of the world. This gospel demands knowledge of itself in terms of the human heart, and deep awareness of that human heart and of ordinary life. It indeed demands ears to hear and eyes to see, to read the signs of the times. And since that is the case, the priest or minister has to be 'relational' and 'functional', though not just in terms of being related or merely performing a function, task or role. Here priesthood and ministry are just as much about what 'is' as they are in the 'essentialist' tradition, but what 'is' is actually a deep core of being within relationships and contexts and so is to be discovered in many different forms.

In this approach theology is something primarily to be *done*, a praxis with reflection coming after. And since the gospel is like this, the priest or minister (and by implication all others with him) is to be utterly human, for how else can he in fact perform his calling? There is also an affirmation of the 'secular'. That does not mean capitulation to secular*ism* and atheism, for separation is still very much a reality, though this is a matter of having to walk separately rather than an institutionalized separation. And indeed this 'walking separately' may ultimately lead, as with Jesus, to the sacrifice of life in martyrdom. That can be the ultimate implication of calling and ordaining, and be just as 'indelible' in its own way.

In this way, then, the priest or minister is called to be simultaneously proclaimer of the kingdom present here and now and so pioneer and upbuilder of community on the one hand, and truly human and truly secular on the other. And it is in rediscovery of this fundamental and original calling that he (and, again, others) will rediscover at the same time his rightful identity in the modern world. Personhood here will be more dominant than priesthood and ministry. Priesthood and ministry will indeed be rediscovered within the human and the secular, within the relational and the contextual. Nor will they be in some 'reduced' form. For here we have a reopening to the full potential and possibility of the gospel made fact in human history, to the rich mystery of humanity in Christ, what Paul calls *koinonia*, and to what Schillebeeckx calls authentic creation faith.

This possibility certainly presents enormous challenges to the clergy and to the presuppositions on which they have been trained. So it is not surprising that in recent 'renewal' and 'revival', many have turned inwards and have hidden away within the structures. Longer term, though, that cannot be enough, for something far more fundamental is in the remaking.

Grass-roots communities

This question of identity takes us on into that of grass-roots communities. While traditional religious communities have largely languished in modern times, other 'basic communities' have significantly mushroomed as a major phenomenon. In the Roman Catholic Church they are particuarly evident in the Third World, where they form out of a concern for liberation and justice; but elsewhere too people simply find themselves without a priest and so become 'basic' communities. For the

Church of England, too, throughout the country there are groups for which experience of community is a priority and also house churches; here, congregations may well find themselves without a vicar, or become just part of a plurality of parishes or a teaming and so are thrown back on their own resources.

On the one hand a group of Christians can be fired with faith, can exhibit the characteristics of the very earliest Christian witness, and can even give their lives; but for all that, they cannot be officially recognized as complete or celebrate the eucharist, the wellspring of their life, because they have no priest. On the other, country and small inner-city congregations can be made to wait upon a vicar as if he were bringing through the lifeline, and he himself can be made into a mere service-taker, like the mass-priest in the Middle Ages, virtually divorced from the community, with all that that means for him and them, both theologically and personally.

The essentialist tradition as represented by Moberly and Congar was again bound to respond in the ways that it has done. In the Roman Catholic Church, where the fresher spirit of the Second Vatican Council has been pushed back by traditionalists, particularly in more recent times, basic communities have been made to toe a line where even the loyalty of local bishops has often been brought near to breaking point.[3] For even though justice, a recurrent theme of these grass-roots communities, has been recognized to be important, 'holiness' has been seen to be even more so. The Brazilian theologian Leonardo Boff was summoned to Rome, as indeed was Schillebeeckx himself.

For both the Roman Catholic Church and the Church of England, where basic communities and house churches have emerged, the main church has usually found itself genuinely unable to respond and has often actually felt threatened. For such communities are regarded as not being 'complete'. What is fundamentally at issue here is the presupposed link between priesthood or ordained ministry and eucharist, rather than ministry seen as leadership and community, and then all else is made to hinge upon this link with the eucharist. So a community or congregation cannot be 'complete' until it has 'received' a priest, i.e. one trained in separation from ordinary human and secular life. A community or congregation cannot be 'complete' unless rooted in that 'otherness' that he will be seen to symbolize and embody.

This outlook has implications for more than just the grass-roots congregations and communities. Those in authority become divorced in one way or another from real people's lives down at the grass roots, the image of priesthood or ordained ministry loses its appeal and becomes unattractive, so that vocations fall. The response to this is often that we should 'pray' more; but while such prayer undoubtedly concentrates the will and takes us into hidden areas from which unknown energies may be unleashed, because it is set within a two-world mentality of separated grace and nature, it can finally do little more than exhaust itself. Its direction and the images to which it is related no longer chime in as once they did with the quite proper major concerns and dreams of people's lives. Just as bad, it blinds those who practise it to the riches of the alternative, which arises out of community and involvement.

Here again the existentialist tradition represented by Schillebeeckx offers quite another possibility. Again it is the gospel with which we are concerned, not as something merely given to the church but, as in the New Testament, as having irrupted into human history as a living reality. Where gospel intersects with the world, it tends naturally to create community, human community which is at the same time both the sacrament and sign of the Spirit of the truly human Jesus and the continuing servant of the cause of God worked through him in human history. According to this tradition, reality is grounded in the grass roots.

In this light the grass-roots communities in the Third World already actualize the gospel, provided that they are in communion with the remainder of the true church. In this light congregations and communities without priest or vicar at least prefigure true churches, if they are not actually so already. In this tradition there is another kind of holiness, this-worldly rather than other-worldly, deeply human, involved in the heights and depths of the world's joys and sorrows, and particularly to be found in a true and faithful following of Jesus, man for others and suffering servant of God. Here priests are not so much 'prayed for' as 'realized', certainly in prayer and by the charisma of the Holy Spirit, but from within the grass-roots community. By virtue of the recognized charism of the Spirit for the leadership of proclamation and building up of community, and by virtue of that alone, they celebrate the eucharist, not as 'getting through to some other world in a holy communion' but as the parting gift of Jesus to the church as God's new covenant people which carries on his cause. That cause is none other than the rich mystery of humanity in Christ, *koinonia*, as Paul calls it, and ultimately that union of the communality of all when God shall be all in all.

If that is the cause, the church must be in touch with all that is human. There can be no place for the accepted tradition of institutionalized separation. Christians must take the gospel to every corner of the world and discover how it will body out and build up community at its points of intersection in the depths and at the edges of ordinary secular life. And while so much of the church seems trapped within fossilized institutions which can by no means legitimately claim to be unchangeable or eternal, do not the grass-roots communities and congregations throughout the world in fact prefigure, if not actually realize, a new coming reality and church of community-in-communities, in Christ?

Celibacy

The two issues of celibacy and the ordination of women again take us to a point of conflict between essentialist and existentialist traditions. Significantly, both issues are about the same matter, sexuality: in the former case this is very obviously sexuality in the physical sense, but more widely also in the separateness of male personality as a whole; in the latter the issue is sexuality in the sense of overall distinctiveness between male and female personality. Both issues are also, however, fundamentally related to the principle which locates reality in 'otherness', 'above' and 'beyond', a principle which has tended to be expressed in terms of maleness, and in particular in those faculties like intellect and abstraction which are traditionally thought to distinguish male from female.

Schillebeeckx records that in its earlier history, celibacy originated in the practice of married priests abstaining from sexual intercourse before celebrating the eucharist,[4] and the desire throughout has undoubtedly been for 'purity' as opposed to what has been felt to be 'impurity' in sex and indeed in all the 'passions of the flesh'. So Catholic documents about celibacy even up to 1954 have referred to the Old Testament levitical laws on 'purity'. Of course this talk about 'purity' need not lead us to think that sex is unclean and dirty, as is often popularly suggested, since it is actually subtle theological language. For all that, however, the terminology must imply a 'rising above' the 'passions of the flesh'.

With a new understanding of sex and sexuality, this approach has proved open to a number of serious criticisms. For example, celibacy, with all its implications not only for priesthood but for church life as a whole, is a practice, whether legally enforced or freely adopted, which has been introduced by men alone and indeed by particular men who have had leadership of the Catholic Church. What are the consequences of this for the life of the *whole* of the body of Christ? Are they healthy ones? Moreover, is not this attitude bound up with the view endorsed by both the Roman Catholic Church and the Church of England that sexuality is primarily for procreation and not for pleasure? (Only in its new 1980 Prayer Book did the Church of England alter the priorities in the aims of marriage in the old service and acknowledge that sexuality had a different character, and then gave the new form as only 'an alternative'.) But is that too, particularly in our modern age, with the widespread availability of birth control and our awareness of the threat of over-population, not too narrow and negative an approach? But here again in the Roman Catholic tradition there is the rigid official position that human contraception is wrong in principle, which no amount of well-reasoned and grounded argument seems capable of changing. So we find a closely interrelated complex of factors each of which has a bearing on another, and again pointing to some deeper underlying problem, which is once more an expression of a two-world mentality of grace and nature, when what is being cried out for is a vision of one world of graced nature.

The alternative to the traditional approach, which I have called 'existentialist', certainly does not rule out celibacy, but it does set it in a very different perspective. Celibacy is now seen as having a very human, personal character, presumably very much as with Jesus. It is rooted in genuine humanness and community, and in deep involvement in these can articulate a mysticism every bit as genuine as the more traditional kind. Because it is personal, it also leaves room for married priests or ordained ministers. For now the gospel is not only not an 'otherness' locked into either an 'eternal' and unchanging church structure or an 'eternal' and unchanging message, depending on whether one is Catholic or Evangelical, but is bodied out afresh within every context of the world, and that obviously includes marriage with all its human consequences.

Such living reality will also be bodied out within the marriage relationship. The implications of this view of the gospel could not be larger. For here there will be the possibility of a mysticism of the marriage relationship. Married priests or ordained ministers may not in one sense be so pastorally 'available' as in the other tradition, but they will bring a significantly different presence to their ministry and the entire life of the church. This has long been recognized in the parish life of the Church of England with the regular call for a 'family man' in the vicarage. Love of God need no longer be seen in sharp contradistinction to love of another person. Human love is raised up from the grass-roots and made holy. The Christian family can become the domestic church which the Second Vatican Council wanted but could not attain because of the force of presuppositions of the kind that we saw with Congar.

This whole area needs to be taken particularly seriously, because it is above all in the sphere of marriage and sexuality that there is the greatest disparity between the actual behaviour of Christians and official teaching;[5] sometimes, even, there is simply no teaching at all because no real theology has grappled with the modern confusions! Here a vision can be created which is now based on the genuinely human and the genuinely personal, freed from the shackles of the merely biological. This is a vision perfectly proper to the gospel, about the dignity of persons, and which from that standpoint and with proper pastoral and common sense can deal with modern dilemmas about marriage,[6] divorce and remarriage, sex and contraception and the wider sphere of medical ethics.

The ordination of women

This issue naturally follows on within the selfsame perspective. Of course the movement for the ordination of women has been influenced by the feminist movement generally, but it would be a serious mistake to dismiss it as simply being feminism in a church context, or merely concerned with equality and rights. Feminism, too, need not of course be merely about equality or rights, which are social realities, but is also most authentically about a person's inner sense of dignity. The crucial point is where the source of that dignity is located. Those women claiming a calling to ordination, pointing beyond mere feminism as being the mere shadow of their concern, clearly locate it within the church. In each age the gospel finds expression through the contemporary secular agenda and its models of understanding and activity, and how could it be otherwise? In this sense the world always sets the agenda for the church. But this claim for new dignity by some women clearly affects the whole church and its entire spirit. For far more than seeking equality across the sexes and putting women where once there were only men, it promises to carry all that is distinctively female, the way that the female distinctively experiences life and the 'dignity' of being Christian into the leadership of the church. If such women as it were remain women and do not merely masquerade as men, the church will indeed be faced with a major revolution in its life. So it is perhaps significant that in modern times the Roman Catholic Church is officially re-emphasizing its doctrine of Mary, picturing womanhood as submissive and that submissive womanhood as being allied to the Godhead.[7]

So the call for the ordination of women is by no means simply a matter of opening up the celebration of the eucharist to women and allowing them to pronounce the absolution of sins as the natural completion of what they already do. Nor is it simply a practical matter of helping to meet the needs of congregations who have no vicar. It has much wider implications than that.

We are familiar with the essentialist tradition of Moberly and Congar. For it, since God chose a man in Jesus for his Christ rather than a woman, since Jesus chose men only for his apostles, since they in turn chose men and not women as their successors, and since the same has been done in unbroken continuity in every succeeding generation, male priesthood has a character which is 'ontological', 'essential', and beyond all history and culture, which are really 'accidental'. We have already noted the presuppositions in this kind of account.

It even seems to extend further, though, into the very understanding of God. Since, it is said, Jesus spoke of God clearly as Father and never as Mother, God seems in some sense 'male'. The Eastern Orthodox Churches, with all their rich tradition of iconography, argue that a priest must be a man, for only so can a priest be a true icon of Christ the man, himself the true icon of God. That makes unity impossible with any church which has women priests. But as we have noted, maleness in a priesthood (particularly a celibate one) is given to idealism and abstraction, so we may well ask whether it has not produced the needs itself. Has it perhaps hypostatized mere abstracts, and then led people to believe that they are realities, turning away from those who are unable to believe this? It is certainly a problem that this whole attitude is by nature divorced, for all its talk of incarnation, from that earthed experience of life which is most naturally embodied in the female.

For the existentialist tradition, on the other hand, since the gospel is about God joined with humanity, and since indeed from within this perspective the significance of Christ as the man Jesus is not as 'God coming as a man' or 'into a man' (so that there have continuingly to be priests or ministers who have to be male) but rather as being a living symbol of God-and-man, God joined with humanity,[8] women priests must be at least a possibility. That is so not least because the gospel has to be bodied afresh from within every new context with its particularities of history and culture, and indeed cannot be gospel unless it does this. So in modern times, in those cultures where women's place has changed from what it was in Jesus' time and where that change expresses a wholly different ethos and context for the gospel, there is good reason for the possibility of their calling to be recognized.

But there is a further point to note. For from this perspective, to think of 'women priests' is a significant contradiction in terms, for here the gospel is about that grace which comes to completion and maturity in a graced nature instead of being separate from it. Priesthood is but one model among many models of response to the mystery of God, as we shall see in the next chapter, and a distinctly 'male' response at that, in the sense of being directed 'out there' and 'up there'. Would not putting women within that mould destroy the gospel from the very first moment? That is a point to which we shall have to return.

But it cannot be an excuse for ruling out the ordination of women in our imperfect world. If 'context' in Western societies is at least characterized by humanizing, human sciences and technology, deeper knowledge of self and of personal and group relationships, the emancipation of women, dreams of community and of one world, yet also by Third World poverty and oppression, the threat of annihilation, nihilism and materialism disintegrated personality, breakdown of relationships, alienation, divisiveness, the need for reconciliation and so on, women ordained to the leadership of the church might perhaps not only bring a more balanced spirit to the church set in that world but, even more, signal that the church was being more truly inspired and given form by a gospel which by definition had to intersect with the world and be bodied out from within it.

Women ordained to leadership would certainly earth gospel and church much more at grass roots, would bring into play the distinctive characteristics of femaleness, and would discern gospel and church much deeper down in the joys and sorrows of humankind. It is no accident that modern psychology accuses many males, especially priests, of a schizoid separating off of the depths of personality and a true experience of life. Femaleness could direct us to a God more naturally given to be suffering servant and crucified one, a vulnerable God for whom life in fact comes through death.

Crisis of numbers

Throughout the previous four issues then – and there could have been more – it has been clear that two diametrically opposed views of life and faith are in conflict. To be more accurate, emphasizing the insight of contextual theology that Christian communities or churches are communities in context, the issues themselves are the visible irruption of the conflict. But it should be equally clear that the conflict experienced from within one view or the other cannot be described in the simplistic terms that we so often hear: God and anti-God, Christ and anti-Christ, doctrine and reductionism, true church and worldliness, reality and indoctrination and so on, for the conflict is between two traditions. Where truth, properly understood, ultimately lies is very hard, if not impossible, to say. What can be said is that each tradition must equally be susceptible to error. A vital check is that truth can be acknowledged only within the tension of duality-within-unity.

However, what we find in our time is not only conflict between two traditions but, as a powerful expression of that conflict, the massive crisis of numbers in priesthood or ordained ministry in all the churches, with the stuntedness of life and personal deprivation that must mean for the church and the continuing suffering and deprivation it must mean for the world which Jesus even died to save. The crucial question is, what are that crisis and conflict about – in simple terms?

Ultimately, I have argued, they are about nothing other than the maintenance of a fundamental 'otherness' in the face of the gospel talk of involvement in the deep experience of existence. In that light cannot the crisis of numbers be seen not only as a crisis but as a *krisis*, that Greek term which expresses a judgment by God in history, here a judgment on his church which has so distorted the gospel that that church must now be broken open. Is not this perhaps the meaning of the experience of many priests or ministers nowadays, let alone of the lay people and the world at large whom inevitably they must influence, if only by default, by virtue of the picture of sheer unreality which they present?

If that is the case, as I believe it is, then we need nothing short of what Juan Luis Segundo, the Latin liberation theologian, has spoken of as the liberation *of* theology, to quote the title of his best-known book. Segundo is speaking from a continent originally colonized and at the same time invaded by a Christianity of Western, Latin culture. But we are all challenged by the same call to throw off the shackles of the Western essentialist tradition to find proper theological reformation of many things, not just priesthood or ordained ministry, but the church and theology as a whole.

Fifth Interlude

'Son of man, prophesy against the shepherds of Israel, prophesy, and say to them, even to the shepherds, Thus says the Lord God: Ho, shepherds of Israel who have been feeding yourselves! Should not shepherds feed the sheep? You eat the fat, you clothe yourselves with the wool, you slaughter the fatlings; but you do not feed the sheep. The weak you have not strengthened, the sick you have not healed, the crippled you have not bound up, the strayed you have not brought back, the lost you have not sought, and with force and harshness you have ruled them. So they were scattered, because there was no shepherd; and they became food for all the wild beasts. My sheep were scattered, they wandered over all the mountains and on every high hill; my sheep were scattered over all the face of the earth, with none to search or seek for them . . . Therefore, you shepherds, hear the word of the Lord: Thus says the Lord God, behold, I am against the shepherds; and I will require my sheep at their hand, and put a stop to their feeding the sheep; no longer shall the shepherds feed themselves. I will rescue my sheep from their mouths, that they may not be food for them.

'For thus says the Lord God: Behold, I, I myself will search for my sheep, and will seek them out. As a shepherd seeks out his flock when some of his sheep have been scattered abroad, so will I seek out my sheep; and I will rescue them from all places where they have been scattered on a day of clouds and thick darkness. And I will bring them out from the peoples, and gather them from the countries, and will bring them into their own land; and I will feed them on the mountains of Israel, by the fountains, and in all the inhabited places of the country. I will feed them with good pasture, and upon the mountain heights of

Israel shall be their pasture; there they shall lie down in good grazing land, and on fat pasture they shall feed on the mountains of Israel. I myself will be the shepherd of my sheep, and I will make them lie down, says the Lord God. I will seek the lost, and I will bring back the strayed, and I will bind up the crippled, and I will strengthen the weak, and the fat and the strong I will watch over; I will feed them in justice.'

Ezekiel 34.2–16 (RSV)

CHAPTER SEVEN

Who is a Priest?

By now it should be abundantly clear that questions about the nature and task of church and theology as a whole, indeed about God, are all naturally interdependent, but that they focus acutely on one particular question. Who is a priest or ordained minister? One tradition answers this question in basically 'essentialist' terms, in terms of status, of a character indelibly imprinted, of grace which is handed down through the apostolic succession, of a focus in terms of 'otherness' and the beyond, of a 'calling' experienced as coming from that 'above-beyond', from God. That tradition goes back a very long way and has been the dominant one in most of the church's history, so much so that it has often given the impression of being the only possible one.

More recently, it has been challenged by what I have called the 'existentialist' tradition, which as represented for example by Schillebeeckx would see priesthood or ordained ministry as rooted in the realities of this world and as coming into being perhaps through identifying experience of God or Jesus which is already present, which has the consequence of issuing in a role of 'leading' the church into proclamation and discovery of the living presence of kingdom in the depths and at the edges of ordinary secular experience, into such human community as may rightfully be said to be living sacrament, that kind of spirituality and holiness actually to be found in genuine deep human goodness and holy joy, of which Paul speaks so eloquently in his letters.

That alternative approach not only challenges a long held understanding of the nature of ministry and priesthood but even more powerfully assaults the very basis on which it stands, its claim to relate to an 'eternal' essence or 'given' nature. For it is associated with theological and historical study which has brought with it awareness that priesthood and ministry, no matter of what kind, has always grown up in history. And such developments can be wrong as well as right. Nor do they go on for ever in the same way: they undergo change, and what has changed in the past can also change in the future.

There is no denying the fact that the gospel, rather than 'descending from heaven', actually irrupted into human history, in human particularity, in the human Jesus of Nazareth. No matter what else was said about him at that time or came to be said about him later, particularly that he was Christ and Lord, Christianity began and continued as something utterly human. And undeniably, it began by taking shape in small communal institutions. Later, its institutional form changed from the cell-like community and the 'community of communities' into a more unified, more hierarchical, more monolithic church, not surprisingly modelled on contemporary social institutions, and particularly imperial institutions, and also took on a system of law which paralleled that of Roman law. Here was a change, for from that point on the Spirit in the church and its whole atmosphere would become 'hierarchical', with all that goes with such an attitude.

It was a historical change, so we may quite legitimately ask questions about it. Was this change a proper new revolution and understanding of the Spirit, or was it on the contrary the loss of the true Spirit within an institutional form utterly inappropriate to its dynamic and utterly stifling to its life? In this change, at that most critical point in the history of the church, was the will of God properly discerned as being that other-worldly holiness located in a hierarchical institution which should from then on be the fundamental basis of the gospel, and even deemed to be 'eternal', or was this a fundamental betrayal of gospel, humanity and suffering world, for all of which Jesus was willing to go even to the cross? If there is no answer to such questions, they are nevertheless haunting, particularly in the face of our modern problems. In this perspective how can there possibly be easy talk about 'true church' and 'false church', and so on? Those who talk so easily in such ways need to learn the gift of silence.

A recognition of the historical dimension poses other problems. If we ask the question 'Who is a priest?' of the New Testament we do not get much of an answer. Perhaps one of the most striking things about the church's earliest attitude is that priestly language is never central and that in no passage of the New Testament is an individual called a priest. Christ may be presented as high priest in the Letter to the Hebrews (7.11–28), but it is undeniable that this is only one image among many, and that here, as in the many other images that the New Testament uses, from pioneer, good shepherd and life of the world to principle and upholder of the universe, it is Christ who defines the image, not the image which defines Christ. Indeed in Hebrews, as must always be the case, Christ is actually breaking the image open, since the reality which is really being discussed is not just priesthood but Christ's being 'for ever'. It is this which mediates a new 'covenant' from God: that is, a new relationship for humankind with God, superseding the old covenant, and priesthood is simply one description among many of this new relationship.

The adjective 'priestly' is used in the New Testament, but it is applied to the people of God as a whole, and the reference is to the general call for holiness as prefigured in the Old Testament and the covenant relationship. The old traditional view that Christ founded a church of priests whose main, perhaps only, function would be to celebrate the eucharist arises out of a wrong reading of the New Testament which is developed in an illegitimate theology and then projected back on to the New Testament in a perspective which distorts what it says.

Even more surprising, perhaps, is that the language of apostleship is no more central to that of the New Testament than that of priesthood. Apostleship is about being sent; the Twelve can in no way be regarded exclusively as the apostles; many others are called apostles, after experiences of the Risen Christ which could in no way be transmitted, generating new communities in their own particular contexts. It is the living gospel and these Christian communities themselves which are apostolic.

Now if neither the language of priestliness nor that of apostleship in the traditional sense are central to the New Testament, what is? It is in fact the language of discipleship. 'That gospel theme becomes the "in Christ" of St Paul, emphasizing that the

context of all ministries is the whole body of the people of God.
All are called to be in Christ; *all* are endowed with gifts of
service for the building up of the Body of Christ; some are called
to exercise their particular gifts of leadership as a service in the
body of Christ. Nor is ministry simply to be equated with
apostleship. The apostles are foundation, are witnesses to the
resurrection. But because they are this, they are irreplaceable,
and continuity with them is continuity with their pastoral care
of the ongoing church rather than succession to their state. The
apostolic group of the Twelve is a centre of unity, a focus of
authenticity for the church, not the source of gifts, which come
from the Holy Spirit. Two words recur: service (*diakonia*) and
gift (*charisma*) – gifts of service, above all service of the word
which grows and spreads in the communion (*koinonia*) of the
churches. The multiplicity of service and proclamation was
very diversely organized in the early days. But the leadership
soon settled (most noticeably in the Pastoral Epistles and Acts)
into the more stable form of elders (presbyters) and overseers
(*episcopoi*). This is secular ("city council") language. It betokens
corporate leadership continuing the work of pastoral care of the
churches "founded" on the "apostles and prophets". Gradually
the *episcopos* emerges as chairman, not just in a secular role *but
with oversight defined by the purposes and concerns of this
unique community of salvation.*'[1]

What is remarkable about the character of this discipleship
and of these unique communities of salvation is that while they
are not 'just secular', they are surprisingly secular. The new
mystery of humanity in Christ remarkably rejects the earlier
Jewish sacredness. Early church fathers distinctly claim that
they do not have a 'sacrifice' and, as we have seen, this causes
them regularly to be accused by contemporary society of being
atheists. Here indeed is the unique reality of graced nature.

If we take with due seriousness this sort of evidence, from the
period before the shift in understanding of ministry and priesthood which was not reversed even at the time of the Reformation, we can then go on to ask further questions. May we not
even ask whether priesthood or ordained ministry is no more
than one model among many of discipleship down Christian
history?

'History suggests that we can ask whether we are to think of the priest as primarily a man endowed with sacred powers to celebrate the eucharist and other sacraments or as a minister of the word. And if we can hold these in tension, what is to be the relation between these godly notions and the more humanly based concept of leader in the community? Is a person leader because ordained as a celebrant of the eucharist and minister of the word, or a celebrant and minister because the appointed leader? And what sort of leadership in what sort of community? Is it to be an omnicompetent sacro-secular leadership in a largely passive community or a more general, co-ordinating, facilitating leadership in a co-responsible group? And is the community to be seen as an ark of salvation in an evil world or as servant of an already redeemed yet still sinful humanity? Finally, is the community to be seen in terms of smaller primary groups (where relationships are primarily affective) or of larger secondary groups (where the relationships are primarily functional)? Answers to these sorts of questions are needed before we can determine what sort of life of the spirit a priest should nourish.'[2] The force of these further words of Joseph Laishley is again to show up the need for us to become aware of our presuppositions and to indicate that we cannot simply remain 'faithful to tradition'. Even there we have to ask the question: which tradition?

What in fact we see from Christian history and from an acknowledgment of our presuppositions is that there can be no one form of the church, and so of priesthood or ministry or leadership, which can rightly be claimed to express the whole truth about the church. We cannot rightly claim an absolute, complete, eternal truth, for all that there certainly seems to be a 'uniqueness' and 'finality' to Christian life. The point is that as that unique life becomes embodied in different situations we inevitably have to deal with forms, and while all of these have had their value, they have also had inadequacies, most notably in the obvious one-sidedness that we have already come across. Leadership of priesthood or ministry has been too detached from its context in the world; it has also been too identified with it. It has been too institutionalized; it has lacked structure. It has insisted on its authority, to the loss of proper human freedom; it has lacked authority, and so on. All forms, then, have been and can only be partial and incomplete, for now we can see only through a glass darkly. Acknowledging this proper view, we can then go on to say that truth is something to be worked out afresh in each new time and place, and this under the control of sensitive dialogue between past history and present concerns. What is our reality? – What was theirs? How did they respond? – How must we? and so on. Tradition is no static thing, fixed for ever, but the stream of living experience and the history of a particular people within the world's history which must be picked up and reworked and carried forward in each new time and place. It is a matter of response, and choice.

But the deeper truth behind recognition of the conflicting notions about priesthood and ministry and the presuppositions underlying them is that they ought all ultimately to be seen within fundamental tensions given in the very nature of existence itself. This is the true perspective from which to judge Christian history and our own present. The most fundamental tension is perhaps that between sacred and secular. All human beings surely have a sense of 'being given' life, a sense perhaps of miracle in the mysteries of life and death, of being called beyond themselves to communion with God. But we can over-interpret this so that it becomes a dualistic two-world mentality with the sacred located in some 'other' world and the secular being seen as pejorative, atheistic, hostile. Or as at present we can see valuable symbols of the sacred being swept away in reaction. Here what we need is not dualism but a proper duality-within-unity of sacred and secular.

Another fundamental tension is that between sacramental presence and eschatological hope. Here again, on the one hand human beings instinctively engage with the ordinary things of life and in so doing may experience them as symbols of the deepest meaning, even perhaps of the presence of God. On the other hand, they also know that all things must pass and that destiny is in some way 'beyond'. So our destiny is both here and not here. But again we can so over-interpret this as to construct a dualistic two-world mentality from it. We can deny the present completely: we can live to the present absolutely. In Christian tradition there has always been the paradox of celebrating God's love and presence on the one hand and renouncing the world in patient waiting, self-denial, fasting, vigil and celibacy on the other. In the past the Christian tradition has often virtually denied the created and creative ordinary gifts of life; in the present time the pendulum is perhaps swinging too far the other way. Here too, the balance needs to be maintained.

And a third fundamental tension is that between individual and corporate forms of leadership. On the one hand is the powerful, pastoral, father figure, being a representative of Christ and leading his people and his flock. On the other is the gentler, self-effacing harmonizer, whose character is found in mutuality, co-operation, supportiveness, affirmation, sensitivity to the gifts of others, facilitating, service. This figure flourishes in smaller groupings, which are affective, while the other figure flourishes in larger groupings which are more functional. It is no idle comment to remark that the former represents more masculine qualities, the latter more feminine, for such an observation focusses so much of the newer spirit abroad, expressed in the calls for women's ordination, for recognition of small grass-roots communities, for relaxation of the rule of celibacy, for rediscovery of church and community and so on. But such an approach is not finding it at all easy to make progress.

However, it cannot be held back much longer. For whatever the 'renewal' and 'growth' and 'fresh spirit' claimed to be there in the traditional churches, whatever the 'corners turned', it seems undeniable that the 'other-worldly' image of church and Spirit and priesthood or ordained ministry is in collapse. A new image is being created, or rather rediscovered, focussed on the here and now, on humanness and personhood and community, on the world at large, particularly as it suffers and longs for wholeness and communion. Here, as we have seen, is the rich mystery of *koinonia*, to be gathered up ultimately in the consummation of a new heaven and a new earth, when God will be all in all.

The church is being called to a fundamental recreation of itself; its self-understanding and its theology, its vision of its authority and life and task, its spirituality and its ethics, its relationship to the world at large, its shape and the way it does its business, down to the most ordinary of details. The church is to be rediscovered primarily through a fresh grasp of itself as community in context, in the context of the wider world as well as the particularity of its own situation, and as founded on the gospel which has intersected with the context. This church will 'proclaim the kingdom', certainly not by words alone, in a world known to be God's creation and, though sinful, yet redeemed. It will speak prophetically of such things as the dignity and freedom of every person, the givenness of things, the power of life and love, of how all life and love come ultimately from God as gift, and by living out such prophetic truths in the utterly human community will naturally discover itself as living sacrament of God and servant of the cause of Jesus.[2]

But of course this rediscovered image will affect most acutely those in positions of leadership, in the priesthood or ordained ministry. The challenge is above all to them, and without their recognition of the tide that is running in their churches the prospect is disastrous and disruptive. It is no longer enough faithfully to celebrate the sacraments and preach the word, faithfully to pray and visit the sick, and to hope somehow to pay the bills. The crisis on all the churches is far more fundamental, going to the very heart of all we do and believe we are to be, but at the same time opening up a new way. I have tried in the previous pages to indicate something of its character, though inevitably the contours are not yet clear. To give an instance of its embodiment in an individual, let me end by quoting Monica Furlong's words about the American monk Thomas Merton: 'As the years stripped away the obvious answers . . . he felt himself to be left with little but his humanity. Like Dietrich Bonhoeffer in his prison he began to see that the highest spiritual development was to be ordinary, to be fully a human being in the way few human beings succeed in becoming, so simple, so naturally themselves.'[3]

NOTES

1 A Time of Change

1. John A. T. Robinson, *The Human Face of God*, SCM Press 1973, cf. Edward Schillebeeckx, *The Church with a Human face*, SCM Press 1985.

2. W. B. Yeats, 'The Second Coming', *Collected Poems*, Macmillan 1950.

2 Recent Problems

1. Jan Kerkhofs, 'From Frustration to Liberation. A Factual Approach to Ministries in the Church', in *Minister! Pastor! Prophet! Grass Roots Leadership in the Churches*, SCM Press 1980, pp. 5f.; cf. *The Right of the Community to a Priest*, *Concilium* 133, 1980. I am indebted to the Kerkhofs article for details of the trend I go on to describe and it should be consulted for individual statistics. These were the latest figures available to me when the research on which this book is based was originally done. The trend may have levelled off a little here and there since, but it is not being reversed and the case still stands.

2. Poland is significant. It is a country with a strong tradition of Catholicism in probably 90% of its population. The church-state relationship there, where the state is officially Communist, has inevitably led to a strong institutional model of the church. Finally, the present Pope was doubtless chosen by the Catholic authorities in hope of strong leadership and regeneration of the church worldwide in a confused and troubled world. Inevitably, however, he has brought into the leadership that conservative, strongly institutional and separated outlook which, while natural enough in Poland, is at odds with that in other parts of the world. Cf. especially Juan Luis Segundo, *Theology and the Church. A Response to Cardinal Ratzinger and a Warning to the Whole Church*, Geoffrey Chapman 1985.

3. John A. Tiller, *A Strategy for the Church's Ministry*, CIO 1983, p. 21.

4. *Minister! Pastor! Prophet!*, pp. 17f.

5. Anthony Russell, *The Clerical Profession*, SPCK 1980.

6. *The Report of the Lambeth Conference*, CIO 1978, p. 54.

7. Victor de Waal, 'What is Ordination?', in *The Sacred Ministry*, ed. Gordon Dunstan, SPCK 1970, p. 88.

8. *Minister! Pastor! Prophet!*, p. 13.

First Interlude

1. Adrian Mitchell, *Poems*, Cape 1964, p. 28.

2. Austin Smith, *Passion for the Inner City*, Sheed and Ward 1983, pp. 119f.

3. Karl Rahner, *Grace and Freedom*, Burns and Oates and Herder and Herder 1969, p. 215; reprinted in *The Practice of Faith*, SCM Press and Crossroad Publishing Co. 1985, p. 111.

3   R. C. Moberly, *Ministerial Priesthood*

1. In his preface to the 1969 reissue of *Ministerial Priesthood*, see below.

2. R. C. Moberly, *Ministerial Priesthood* (1897), second edition John Murray 1899, from which the quotations are taken. Reissued SPCK 1969 with a preface by A. T. Hanson. Page references for individual quotations are given in the text.

Second Interlude

1. Paraphrase by Richard Wheatcroft of a parable by Theodore O. Wedel which appeared in his article 'Evangelism – the Mission of the Church to Those Outside Her Life', *The Ecumenical Review*, October 1953. Quoted by Howard Clinebell, *Basic Types of Pastoral Care and Counselling*, SCM Press and Abingdon Press 1984, pp. 13f.

2. John Bowden, *Edward Schillebeeckx. Portrait of a Theologian*, SCM Press and Crossroad Publishing Co. 1983, pp. 152f.

4   Yves Congar, *Lay People in the Church*

1. Yves Congar, *The Wide World My Parish*, Darton, Longman and Todd 1961.

2. B. C. Butler, *The Theology of Vatican II*, Darton, Longman and Todd 1967, pp. 5f.

3. For the new approach cf. the Vatican Constitution *Lumen Gentium*, in Austin Flannery (ed.), *Vatican II*, Fowler Wright 1981.

4. The first English edition of Yves Congar, *Lay People in the Church*, was published by the Bloomsbury Publishing Company in 1957; it was reissued by Geoffrey Chapman and the Newman Press in 1959, and subsequently in a revised and expanded edition by Geoffrey Chapman in 1964 and the Newman Press in 1965. The page references are to this edition.

Third Interlude

1. Martin Buber, *Between Man and Man*, Collins 1961, p. 33.

2. Karl Rahner, *The Love of Jesus and the Love of Neighbour*, St Paul's Publications and Crossroad Publishing Co. 1983, pp. 69–71; reprinted in

The Practice of Faith, SCM Press and Crossroad Publishing Co. 1985, p. 120.

5 Edward Schillebeeckx, *The Church with a Human Face*

1. John Bowden, *Edward Schillebeeckx. Portrait of a Theologian*, SCM Press and Crossroad Publishing Co. 1983.
2. Edward Schillebeeckx, *God Among Us*, SCM Press and Crossroad Publishing Co. 1983, p. 96.
3. For Schillebeeckx's view of Jesus see his *Jesus. An Experiment in Christology*, Collins and Crossroad Publishing Co. 1979.
4. *God Among Us*, p. 96.
5. Both books were published in Britain by SCM Press and in the USA by Crossroad Publishing Co.
6. Cf. *Ministry*, pp. 100f.; *Church with a Human Face*, p. 8f.
7. For this insight into story see especially *God Among Us*, pp. 232–48.

Fourth Interlude

1. Bertrand Russell, *Autobiography*, Allen and Unwin 1967, Prologue, Vol. I, p. 13.
2. Austin Smith, *Passion for the Inner City*, Sheed and Ward 1983, pp. 7f. The quotation is from Jacques Maritain, *The Range of Reason*, Bles 1953, pp. 121f.

6 Towards New Ministry, Priesthood and Church

1. Edward Schillebeeckx, *The Church with a Human Face*, pp. 8f.
2. See above, pp. 23f.
3. *Minister! Pastor! Prophet!*, p. 20; *The Church with a Human Face*, p. 209ff.
4. *The Church with a Human Face*, pp. 240ff.
5. Walter Kasper, *Theology of Christian Marriage*, Burns and Oates 1980, p. 1f.
6. Cf. Joseph Laishley, 'Marriage and the Family', *The Way*, April 1983, pp. 87–95. Kasper and Laishley convincingly restate the marriage bond in terms of personal relationship, dignity and potential which is God's potential for marriage, rather than as something indelibly stamped upon two people, and so make it a challenging moral responsibility. A different sacramental theology is entailed, genuinely sacramental rather than sacral and juridical.
7. Chapter 8 of *Lumen Gentium* is devoted entirely to Our Lady, Austin Flannery, *Vatican II*, pp. 413–23.
8. Cf. F. W. Dillistone, 'Male-Female Symbolism', in Hugh Montefiore (ed.), *Yes to Women Priests*, Mayhew-McCrimmon 1978.

7 Who is a Priest?

1. Joseph Laishley, 'Spirituality and Priesthood', *The Way*, Summer

1983, pp. 4f. I wish to acknowledge my debt in this chapter to a seminar group held at Heythrop College, London, in 1984, led by Dr Laishley.

2. Thomas Cullinan, *Eucharist and Politics*, CIIR 1974, p. 299.
3. Monica Furlong, *Merton: A Biography*, Collins 1980, p. xviii.